D1165409

T 21

English Land Measuring to 1800:
Instruments and Practices

Publications in the series include:

History of the Lathe to 1850
Robert S. Woodbury

English Land Measuring to 1800: Instruments and Practices
A. W. Richeson

The Development of Technical Education in France 1500–1850
(in preparation)
Frederick B. Artz

English Land Measuring to 1800:
Instruments and Practices

A. W. Richeson

PUBLISHED JOINTLY BY

The Society for the History of Technology

AND

The M.I.T. Press

MASSACHUSETTS INSTITUTE OF TECHNOLOGY
CAMBRIDGE, MASSACHUSETTS, AND LONDON, ENGLAND

Preface

The present work on the history of English land measuring was first suggested to the author by a study of the terms and units used by the Saxons in the division and distribution of the conquered lands to their followers after the invasion of England.

This history of surveying presents the development of land measuring in England from its origin in pre-Roman times through 1800. Although emphasis is upon the development of the science of surveying and the construction of the necessary instruments for its conduct, human activities closely related to surveying are also discussed. Throughout the manuscript an attempt has been made to demonstrate the slow changes in the methods of surveying, influenced in part by a changing condition in land ownership and tenure, and the gradual improvement in instrument construction from Humphrey Cole in the sixteenth century to Jesse Ramsden and others by the close of the eighteenth century. Likewise we will examine the effects of the improvment of education, higher living standards, land enclosing, agricultural reforms, and many other factors upon the development of surveying from Saxon Britain to the close of the eighteenth century.

PREFACE

I want to thank my friends and colleagues who have offered suggestions and criticisms in what has been a long task. I particularly want to thank I. Bernard Cohen, Professor of the History of Science and General Education at Harvard University, Derek J. de Solla Price, Professor of the History of Science at Yale University, Thomas Pyles, Professor of English at the University of Florida, Richard H. Shryock, Librarian of the American Philosophical Society, the late Sidney Painter, Professor of History at The Johns Hopkins University, and Melvin Kranzberg, Professor of History at Case Institute of Technology and Editor-in-Chief of *Technology and Culture,* who gave unstintingly of their time for encouragement, suggestions, and aid in conducting the research for the text. I also thank the many librarians and museum directors throughout the world who cheerfully assisted me in procuring photographs of instruments, microfilms of early surveying texts, and abstracts of rare books and manuscripts. However, I am solely responsible for the style, arrangement, and accuracy of the text.

I wish to express my appreciation to the American Philosophical Society for two grants in aid for research, and, finally, to the Research Board of the University of Maryland for a grant to assist in the publication of the manuscript.

College Park, Maryland　　　　　　　A. W. Richeson
January 1966

Editor's Note

The untimely death of Professor Richeson occurred while his manuscript was in proof. The editor of the series and the M.I.T. Press take full responsibility for any errors persisting in the proof.　　　　　　　Melvin Kranzberg

Cleveland, Ohio
April 1966

Contents

Preface   *v*

CHAPTER ONE

Introduction   *1*

    The Need for Land Measurements
    Problems of the Early Surveyor
    Ancient Surveying
    Continental Europe before the Sixteenth Century
    Ancient and Medieval Contributions

CHAPTER TWO

Land Measuring in England from the Saxons
through the Fifteenth Century   *15*

    General Background
    The Anglo-Saxon Land Divisions
    The Norman Conquest
    Agriculture and Land Tenure
    The Educational Movement
    Anglo-Norman Surveying
    Summary

CHAPTER THREE

The First Half of the Sixteenth Century   29
General Conditions
Sixteenth-Century Surveying Texts
Master Fitzherbert
Richard Benese
Summary

CHAPTER FOUR

The Second Half of the Sixteenth Century   43
General Conditions
Leonard Digges and His Instruments
Humphrey Cole, Instrument Maker
Valentine Leigh
Edward Worsop
Cyprian Lucar
Ralph Agas
Circular Divisions
The Close of the Century

CHAPTER FIVE

The Seventeenth Century   90
Educational Background
John Norden
Arthur Hopton
Aaron Rathborne
William Leybourn
John Eyre
George Atwell
Vincent Wing
Adam Martindale
John Love

CONTENTS

Mathematical Instruments: The Vernier
The Telescope
The Micrometer
The Stadia
Levels: Leveling
Summary of Seventeenth-Century Developments

CHAPTER SIX

The Eighteenth Century   *142*

General Background
Instrument Construction during the First Half of the
    Eighteenth Century
Surveying Texts of the First Half of the Eighteenth
    Century
Second Half of the Eighteenth Century
Minor Publications
Arthur Burns
Summary of Eighteenth-Century Surveying Methods
George Graham
John Bird
The Achromatic Lens
The Stadia
Dividing by Instrument during the Late Eighteenth
    Century
Jesse Ramsden
Topographical Surveys during the Eighteenth Century
The Great Triangulation at Hounslow Heath
Summary and Conclusions

Selected Bibliography   *189*
Index   *209*

Table of Book-Title Abbreviations

Country-Survey	Adam Martindale, *The Country-Survey-Book: or Land-Meter's Vademecum* (London, 1682).
DNB	*Dictionary of National Biography* (Oxford, 1885–1939).
History	David Eugene Smith, *History of Mathematics* (Boston, 1923–1925).
Introduction	George Sarton, *Introduction to the History of Science* (Baltimore, 1927–1947).
Mathematical Practitioners	E. G. R. Taylor, *The Mathematical Practitioners of Tudor and Stuart England* (Cambridge, 1954).
OED	*Oxford English Dictionary* (Oxford, 1933).
Short Title Catalogue	Alfred W. Pollard and G. R. Redgrave, *A Short Title Catalogue of Books Printed in England, Scotland and Ireland and British Books Printed Abroad, 1475–1640* (London, 1926)
Tectonicon	Leonard Digges, *A Booke Named Tectonicon* (London, 1556).

Introduction

The Need for Land Measurements

Nomadic tribes have no need for land measurements. Division of the lands of a primitive people does not become a necessity until the society has reached the level of settled agricultural development. Whenever the population reaches a point at which competition arises for the available land suitable for cultivation, then the demand arises for some form of land division and a means of recording the plots of land belonging to the individual holder.[1]

From the standpoint of the individual landholder, cadastral surveying, that is, surveying carried out for the cadastre, roughly defined as the land register or office, is the most important of the many types of land measurements[2] included in the general term "surveying." The main purpose of cadastral surveys is the demarcation of landed properties, giving the area, boundaries, value, location, and ownership of each individual holding or lot. Records of these surveys serve

[1] Sir Henry G. Lyons, "Ancient and Modern Land Measurements," *The Geographical Teacher*, *13* (1925), 425–432.

[2] Reginald Middleton and Osbert Chadwick, *A Treatise on Surveying*, ed. by W. Fisher Cassie, 6th ed. (New York, 1956), Vol. 2, pp. 366–379.

I

a dual purpose: they verify owners' rights to possession of property, and they afford the state a basis for purposes of taxation. During ancient and medieval times these surveys also gave a record of servitude, stating the rights of the individual serfs attached to the soil as well as the military services that might be required from the overlord of the community.

Problems of the Early Surveyor

Many problems confronted the ancient surveyor; some of these he was able to resolve but others he left for later generations to solve. The ancient surveyor lacked all types of reliable measuring instruments. For measurements of length he used cords and rods of uncertain length whose units had not been standardized. Consequently any given measure might be of uncertain value to all except the surveyor or measurer who performed the operation.

Angle measurements were used but little by the ancient surveyor. The problems of constructing linear scales with a low degree of accuracy were great, but those encountered in the construction of circular scales were for the most part insurmountable. Furthermore, the lack of a suitable direction-finding instrument also added to the surveyor's difficulty.

For leveling, the instruments were almost as nonexistent as those for angle measurements. One of the earliest instruments used for leveling was the isosceles, or "A" type frame, with a plumb bob. In the later part of the ancient period, crude forms of the water level were devised and used with some success.

Ancient records do not indicate that there was any important discussion of the art and methods of surveying before the late Greek and early Roman periods of history. Each individual surveyor probably used a method of surveying which he had devised by trial and error or had learned as an apprentice from his master. Likewise, the records of the survey were poorly recorded, if recorded at all, generally on papyri or clay tablets. These records when available give little pertinent information regarding the instruments used or methods of conducting the survey.

Ancient Surveying

Evidences of the early practice of some form of cadastral surveying have been found in the fertile valleys and plains of the Tigris, Euphrates, and Nile rivers.[3] Some of the earliest records of a form of land measurement are found on the clay tablets of the Sumerians who inhabited the plains between the Tigris and the Euphrates rivers.[4] Numerous extant clay tablets show the plans of cities and agricultural areas nearby these cities. In addition to the clay tablets, boundary stones, used to mark off the boundaries of plots of land, have been preserved. Many of these tablets and boundary stones existed before 1000 B.C.[5]

During the same period, surveying was also taking place in Egypt along the Nile valley. Records of these surveys, giving the dimensions, area, quality, and dues required of the property, are frequently found recorded on the walls of the tombs of prominent Egyptians. Inscriptions from the walls of the Theban tomb of Menna (*ca.* 1400 B.C.) give

[3] Edward Chiera, *They Wrote on Clay* (Chicago, 1938), pp.1–50; George Sarton, *A History of Science* (Cambridge, 1952), Vol. 1. pp. 57–99.

[4] See the Mesopotamian collection in the Museum of the University of Pennsylvania.

[5] William J. Hinkle, *A New Boundary Stone of Nebuchadnezzar I* (Philadelphia, 1907), pp. 116–160.

an idea of the instruments used in these surveys.[6] A few crude instruments of the Sumerians and Egyptians, such as cords, rods, and possibly one or two sighting instruments, were borrowed or copied by the Greeks in their surveys.

Hero of Alexandria, an outstanding Greek mechanician and scientist (fl. *ca.* A.D. 100), was a practical scientist whose works show Egyptian influence.[7] His contribution to surveying was his *Treatise on the Dioptra*, wherein he enunciates the first principles of engineering and surveying. This is without doubt the earliest extant book to be written on surveying; here the fundamental principles of surveying land originated. Hero also gives a description of an instrument called the *dioptra* which, if constructed, was not put to any practical use at that time.[8]

The corpora in the late Greek, or Graeco-Roman, period are rather complete with respect to land measuring. These records give pertinent and detailed information of the dimensions, ownership, and the quality of the land. They also indicate the transfer of the Greek methods and instruments of surveying to the Romans.[9]

[6] Alan H. Gardiner, "The Inscriptions of Mes," *Untersuchungen zur Altertumskunde Aegyptens*, 4 (1905), 1–51; Victor Loret, "Les Grandes Inscriptions de Mes à Saqqarah," *Zeitschrift für Aegyptische Sprache*, 49 (1901), 1–10; François Thureau-Dangin, "Un Cadastre Chaldéen," *Revue d'Assyrologie et d'Archéologie Orientale*, 4 (1897), 13–20.

[7] W. A. Trusdale, "The First Engineer," *Journal Association of Engineering Societies*, 19 (1897), pp. 1 ff.; Herman Schone, "Die Dioptra des Herons," *Archäologisches Institut des Deutschen Reichs*, 16 (1900); and the article "Dioptra" in Pauly-Wissowa, *Real-Encyclo-pädie der classischen Altertumswissenschaft* (Stuttgart, 1905), Vol. 5.

[8] A. G. Drachmann, "Hero's Instruments," *History of Technology*, ed. by Charles Singer *et al.* (Oxford, 1957), Vol. 3, pp. 609–611; E. Lancaster-Jones, "Criticism of Hero's Dioptra," *The Geographical Journal*, 69 (1927), 140.

[9] Otto Neugebauer, "Exact Science in Antiquity," *University of Pennsylvania Bicentennial Conference* (Philadelphia, 1941), pp. 23–31; and George Sarton, *Introduction to the History of Science* (Balti-

In contrast to the Greeks, the Romans exhibited the same characteristics in surveying that they exhibited in mathematics and science in general; that is, they were interested only in the practical. They borrowed from the Egyptians and the Greeks those instruments that they needed in surveying, engineering, and war; and they adapted the abstract geometry of the Greeks to their practical needs in surveying and engineering. Some of the instruments were improved by the Romans, but others were used in almost the exact form of the originals.

In their land measurements the Romans used a variety of instruments, and it is not always possible to determine whether a given instrument was used wholly for engineering purposes, such as the construction of roads, irrigation, and canal work, or was used partly for engineering and partly for land surveying. The Roman line-measuring instruments consisted of wooden rods, cords, and possibly some form of taximeter which may have been developed by Vitruvius (fl. *ca.* 15 B.C.).

For leveling, the Romans developed and adopted instruments of two kinds: those depending on the principle that the surface of a liquid in repose is horizontal, and those depending on the principle that lines perpendicular to a vertical line are horizontal. Instruments of the first type were called the *chorobates* and consisted of a trough partly filled with a liquid, usually water. Instruments of the second type were frequently constructed with a plumb bob and were developed as modified dioptras.[10]

---

more, 1927), Vol. 1, pp. 193–194. (Hereafter referred to as Sarton, *Introduction*.)

[10] Edward Noble Stone, "Roman Surveying Instruments," *University of Washington Publications, 4* (1928), 215–248; F. Blume, K. Lachmann, and A. Rudorff, *Die Schriften der Romischen Feldmesser* (Berlin, 1848).

Ancient surveying reached its peak of perfection with the Romans: the Romans borrowed and improved the instruments of the Egyptians and the Greeks; they constructed new instruments and developed new methods of surveying. After the fall of Rome, many of these instruments and methods survived and were improved during the fourteenth and fifteenth centuries by the instrument makers and mathematical practitioners of continental Europe.[11]

Continental Europe before the Sixteenth Century

Of all the instruments developed during the late Middle Ages, the magnetic compass was of greatest importance to the surveyor. Recent research by Joseph Needham[12] has shown that the Chinese were using the magnetic compass in surveys for cartography in the eleventh century, and we may reasonably suppose that they knew of its attractive properties long before this date. The earliest European reference to the nautical use of the magnetic needle is by Alexander Neckham (1157–1217), an Englishman, about A.D. 1180.[13] There may have been one or two earlier references but they are not authoritative. What is probably the first technical description of the compass was given by a French soldier known as Peter Peregrinus. In his letter on the magnet

[11] For a discussion of the spread of culture during the Middle Ages consult the following: Arthur C. Howland, "The Institutional Pattern of the Middle Ages: Inheritance and Legacy," *University of Pennsylvania Bicentennial Conference* (Philadelphia, 1941), pp. 60–75; Sarton, *Introduction*, Vol. 1, pp. 503–587; Sarton, *Ancient Science and Modern Civilization* (Lincoln, 1924), pp. 1–381; H. J. J. Winter, *Eastern Science: An Outline of its Scope and Contributions* (London, 1952).

[12] Joseph Needham, *Science and Civilization in China* (Cambridge, 1959), Vol. 3, pp. 567–576.

[13] Sarton, *Introduction*, Vol. 2, p. 385; Alexander Neckham, *De Naturis Rerum*, ed. by Thomas Wright (London, 1863), pp. I–XIV–XXXVII, and 98–102.

(*Epistola ad Sygerum de Foucaucourt Militem de Magnete*), he describes not only the floating type of compass but also the fixed or pivotal type, pointing out the distinction between the two poles.

About 1300 the pivoted needle was fixed to a card, which was first divided into eight parts. The original eight-point card was divided into 16 and finally into 32 parts, all of which represented the various winds. About 1500 the fleur-de-lis for the North point on the card was used, while the Frankish initials of the winds, *N, NNE, NE*, etc., were no doubt first used by Flemish navigators.[14]

Modifications were made on the magnetic compass by the Italians, so that land maps could be constructed by compass bearings and distances could be measured from a fixed point. This method of position fixing is illustrated by Niccolo Tartaglia (1506–1557) in his *Quesiti et Inventioni*, published in 1546 at Venice. In the *Quesiti*, Tartaglia describes two instruments of the compass type (Fig. 1) which were either developed by him or constructed under his supervision. The form with the compass inset on the side was the most common, while the second with the compass centrally located was probably more difficult to construct but was more convenient to use since the graduations were larger. The scale graduations were in 64 points, rather than sexagesimal units.

With the development of a compass that could be used for direction location on land, there arose an increased

[14] Sylvanus P. Thompson, "The Rose of the Winds; The Origin and Development of the Compass Card," *Proceedings of the British Academy* (London, 1913–1914); Heinrich Winter, "What is the Present Stage of Research in Regard to the Development of the Compass in Europe?" *Research and Progress*, 2 (1936), 225–233; Charles Singer, Derek J. Price, and E. G. R. Taylor, "Cartography, Survey, and Navigation to 1400," *History of Technology*, ed. by Charles Singer et al. (Oxford, 1957), Vol. 3, pp. 516–529.

ouer trafguardo, fara girabile, cioe che la fe potra girare per ogni uerfo a torno
à torno, & per quelli dui bufettini che faranno in quelle due lamette quadrã
gole in alto elleuate, fe potra trafguardar con uno occhio li fegni, & termini
che fi uora uedere, come per lauenire p effempio fe moftrara, uero è che in luof
co de quelli dui bufettini à mi me piace, et me pare anchora piu fpediéte, due

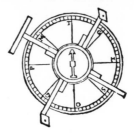

Q V I N T O   65

la iftremita del brazzo. c. d. ui fe potra incaffar, & incollar el brozzetto. e f. &
fquadro come nella foprafcritta figura appare. Et dapoi quefto nel Centro di
tal dioptra bifogna fa ui un bu,ettino & con un pironcino di ferro, ouer di ot
tone piantare tal dioptra nel centro di tal iftromento, laqualcofa facendo tal
iftromëto ftara precife come di fotto appai in figura, et di auefto uene potreti

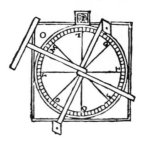

Fig. 1. Tartaglia's compasses. From Tartaglia's *Quesiti et Inventioni*.
    (Courtesy of the Library of Congress.)

8

interest in the construction of maps to be used with direction-finding instruments. In 1511 Waldseemüller (1470–1518) published two maps of the Lorraine and Rhine valleys which indicate that some form of instrument was used in determining direction. An instrument that involved all the necessary characteristics for use with maps of this type is shown by Gregorius Reisch (1471–1528) in the encyclopedia called the *Margareta Philosophica*. This instrument (Fig. 2), called the *Polimetrum* by Waldseemüller, was capable of giving the combined altitude and azimuth reading; an examination shows that the polimetrum was a prototype of the theodolite.

One of the greatest advances in cartography and surveying methods was made by Gemma Frisius (1508–1555) when he enunciated the first principles of his method of triangulation in 1529.[15] In 1533 Gemma Frisius had bound with the Flemish edition of Apian's *Cosmographia* the first edition of his work, the *Libellus*. In the *Libellus*, Gemma gives a detailed description of the method of surveying a large area, a kingdom, or a whole country by triangulation. Gemma considers his method an entirely new method of surveying.[16] In order to accomplish his surveys with triangulation, he devised an instrument called the *epipedometron*, consisting of a modified astrolabe with a compass inset. R. T. Gunther[17]

[15] Extracts on the method of triangulation from the *Libellus* of Gemma Frisius are given by E. G. R. Taylor, *Tudor Geography 1485–1583* (London, 1930), pp. 144–148; and E. G. R. Taylor, "The Earliest Account of Triangulation," *Scottish Geographical Magazine*, 43 (1927), 341–345.

[16] A method of triangulation similar in every respect to that of Gemma Frisius was developed before 1547 by August Hirschvogel (1488–1553). Sigmund Wellisch, "Die Erfindung der Triangulierung," *Zeitschrift des Oesterr. Ingenieur- und Architekten-Vereines*, 20 (1899), 355 ff.

[17] Note following a paper by Miss Taylor on "William Bourne," *The Geographical Journal*, 72 (1938), 339.

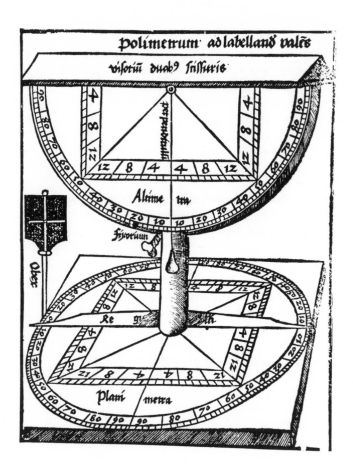

Fig. 2. The polimetrum of Waldseemüller from Gregorius
Reisch's *Margarita Philosophica.*
(Courtesy of the Library of Congress.)

has pointed out that Gemma was fortunate in having several nephews who were instrument makers. One of these, Gualterius Arsenius, was among the first instrument makers to construct an astrolabe with a compass inset, probably under the supervision of Gemma Frisius. Gunther also suggests that these instruments were probably the forerunners of the instruments later made by the illustrious English instrument maker Humphrey Cole (*ca.* 1520–*ca.* 1591).

Although these developments in instruments and methods constituted a great advance in instrument construction, the average surveyor did not have sufficient mathematics at his command to make use of either the methods of triangulation or the instruments to apply these methods. In order to meet this need—that is, to construct an instrument that could be used as a sort of rule-of-thumb method of operation—the plane table and sight rule were developed. Probably the earliest stage in the development of the plane table and sight rule was the *holometer* (Fig. 3) of Abel Foullon. An account of the instrument was published in Paris by Foullon in 1551 with the title, *Usaige et description de l'holomêtre*, and since the name of an instrument maker was given from whom the holometer could be obtained, the instrument apparently did not merely exist on paper. Foullon's illustrations are somewhat difficult to understand because of the poor perspective of the drawings; however, he does give a good description of the instrument which can be followed from the diagram.

In discussing the holometer, E. G. R. Taylor states that the fitting of a piece of paper to the top of the table with fixed scales, rules, and compass inset was certainly a difficult business; on the other hand, the substitution of a "plain" table and a movable sight rule would certainly suggest itself to a practical man.[18]

---

[18] E. G. R. Taylor, "The Plane Table in the Sixteenth Century," *The Scottish Geographical Magazine, 45* (1929), 205–211. According to Taylor, the word *plain* was used for the table as we know it today.

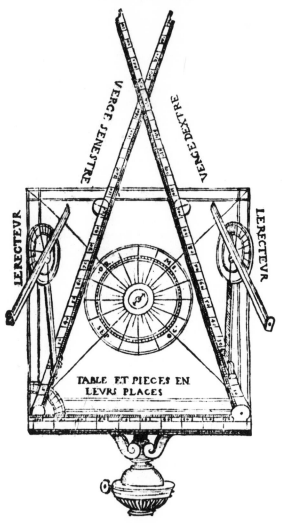

Fig. 3. The holometer of Foullon from Abel Foullon's *l'Holo-mètre*.
(Courtesy of the Library of Congress.)

A great contribution of Abel Foullon was the method of direct drawing of the measurements on a table in the field while the work was in progress. Taylor also points out that the evidence, though not direct, is rather conclusive that the combined "yerge" and "recteur" was the first sight rule to be used.[19] In any case, the holometer of Foullon was certainly an advance in instrument construction and design.

Ancient and Medieval Contributions

By the close of the fourteenth century there had been a slow but steady growth in the art of surveying. Instrument construction during the ancient period had progressed far in advance of that used by the primitive land measurer. This is especially true in line measuring, where the Romans had developed various rods with definite lengths within their system of units. They had also devised and used successfully the water level and levels of the plumb-bob type. Angle measurements had not progressed to any great extent, although Hero of Alexandria had, at least, given in the dioptra the fundamental idea of an angle-measuring instrument.

For the methods of surveying, the defining rules for a survey had been given by Hero in his work on the dioptra. From the writing of the Roman surveyors it is possible to recognize that they had formulated a fairly definite procedure in conducting their surveys. Likewise, there are some instances of a really definite procedure for recording the results of the survey.

Instrument development and construction was the primary contribution of Continental Europe to surveying through the fourteenth and fifteenth centuries. An improved magnetic compass could now be used on land to determine the

[19] Taylor, *op. cit.*, p. 208.

direction of one or more points from a fixed point. In addition to the compass, instruments similar to the polimetrum were developed to give altitude and azimuth readings. Construction of the holometer was significant in that it provided a simple instrument for use in the field for the preparation of a plan or plot of the survey. Gemma Frisius' method of triangulation was the most important contribution to the methods of surveying developed during this period.

These instruments and new methods of surveying were to have a far-reaching effect on English surveying during the sixteenth century.

Land Measuring in England from the Saxons through the Fifteenth Century

General Background

Some form of agriculture certainly existed in Britain before the Roman invasion of Britain. To what extent land measuring was practiced by the original inhabitants, the Celts, is impossible to state with any degree of certainty. We may assume that the instruments and methods used were of a primitive and crude sort.[1]

Available records in England do not indicate any great advance in land measuring after the Romans settled there.[2] It is probable that the Romans brought with them some of the land-measuring instruments and methods that they were accustomed to use in Rome and other parts of Europe. However, we have little or no information to state with certainty

[1] C. S. and C. S. Orwin, *The Open Fields* (Oxford, 1954), pp. 175–179; E. Cecil Curwen, *Plow and Pasture* (New York, 1953), pp. 75–79.
[2] R. G. Collingwood and J. N. L. Myres, *Roman Britain and the English Settlements* (Oxford, 1949), pp. 1–30.

that the Britons were influenced to any appreciable extent by Roman land measuring.[3]

The Anglo-Saxon Land Divisions

Raiding parties and settlers from northern Europe were attracted to parts of Britain long before the invasion of the island by Julius Caesar. From A.D. 287 to the great raid in A.D. 367, and thereafter, the raids and settlements became more frequent and permanent until Roman Britain was completely submerged by the Saxons. Within two or three centuries, the greater part of Britain, with the exception of the West and Southwest, was completely dominated by the peoples from northern Europe, chiefly Anglo-Saxons.

The Saxon settlers in England developed the open-field system of cultivation and the use of the heavy plow. This plow probably consisted of a wheel, a coulter, a plowshare, and a moldboard; in heavy soils the plow was often pulled by as many as eight oxen. Such extensive equipment made individual ownership impossible, and the solution of the problem was the formation among the Saxon peasants of a common plow team. In the group each peasant did not necessarily own his plow and team of oxen as a modern farmer might. One had a plow, while others had one or more oxen which they contributed to the formation of the team, and with this common plow team the peasants plowed in turn the land apportioned to each of the contributors.[4]

In order to facilitate this communal plowing and to apportion the land justly among the workers, the arable lands were divided into strips of suitable widths and lengths for

[3] Collingwood and Myres, *op. cit.*, pp. 208–226; Orwin, ref. 1, pp. 22–26.

[4] H. E. Gray, *English Field Systems* (Cambridge, 1915), pp. 1–568; Orwin, ref. 1, pp. 21–22.

plowing and cultivation. These strips were frequently referred to as *lands* and were grouped into blocks of various sizes called *furlongs*. The arrangement of the furlongs over the fields was not regular, and consequently a field had the appearance of a patchwork quilt. In reality the furlongs were of various lengths and widths depending on the contour of the land, the condition of the soil, and the need for drainage. One or more of these strips usually constituted a day's plowing, and the strips were apportioned among the contributors of the common team in a fairly systematic fashion over the entire field. This method of apportioning the arable land among the workers developed what is frequently referred to as the *open-field* system of cultivation.[5]

Along with the strip method of division and open-field system of cultivation, the Saxons developed a variety of land measures of length and superficial area. The inch and foot do not seem to have had a significant role in the early Anglo-Saxon land measures.

From the standpoint of the early land measurers, the *rod* was the most important lineal unit of measure. There are four related words of almost identical meanings; the *rod*, *rood*, *pole*, and *perch*.[6] Of these terms, the rod and rood were used most often in the late Saxon period, while through the Middle English period the pole and perch were used with the same meaning as the rod. The term "rood," however, was generally, though not always, applied at this time to an area of land rather than to a lineal measure. In the late Saxon period, "rood" was used in the special sense of a distance measure in defining the boundaries of the acre and

[5] Curwen, ref. 1, pp. 84–89; Gray, *op. cit.*, pp. 50–100.
[6] The words "rood" and "rod" are no doubt both derived from the Old Saxon *roda* and later Anglo-Saxon *rod* meaning a rod or pole. "Pole" is from the Anglo-Saxon *pol*, stake, stick, or rod, and was borrowed from the Latin. The term "perch" came through the French from the Latin *pertica*. (*Oxford English Dictionary*, Oxford, 1933).

17

half-acre strips which made up the fields in the open-field system of agriculture. At all times the term rod has been used not only as a lineal unit but also as a unit of superficial area. The late Old English and Middle English *rodd* certainly meant a stick with which to measure, although many references indicate that the term was used to represent surface area as well as length.[7]

During the late Saxon and Early English period the rod, pole, or perch was of various lengths in different parts of the country, varying from 12 feet in southern England to 22 feet in the North. However, in many places throughout England rod measures of different length were used in the same district to measure various types of land. For example, in many places a 12-foot rod was used for arable lands, an 18-foot rod was used for meadows, and a 20- or 22-foot rod was used for rock land and woodland. These rod measures were referred to as *customary rods*, and the acres derived from these measures were called *customary acres* in order to differentiate them from the later *statute acres* measured with the statute rod.[8] These customary rods and acres were used through the eighteenth century and possibly to some extent as late as the nineteenth century in surveying in England.

From the earliest times until the present, the fundamental measure of superficial area in England has been the *acre*. It is true that in some cases the acre has been used in a limited sense as a unit of length, but in general it has always been used to express superficial area.[9]

[7] *Rolls of Parliament* (1502), Vol. 5, p. 59, Col. 1; John Stubbs, *The Discovery of Gaping Gulf* (London, 1579), Folio iii.

[8] C. M. Watson, *British Weights and Measures* (London, 1910), pp. 50–110; Edward Nicholson, *Men and Measures* (London, 1912), pp. 30–185.

[9] Cf. Coverdale Bible, I Samuel XV, 14.

The word acre is derived from the Old English *æcer*, meaning field, and is closely related to the German *Acker*, meaning field or arable land.[10] The term was originally defined as a measure of land as large as a yoke of oxen could plow in a day. In Anglo-Saxon the acre was always 160 square rods, regardless of the length of the rod being used as a measure.[11]

By the close of the Saxon period, few advances had been made in the art of surveying. We know little of the instruments and methods used by the Saxons in their land measurements, but it is certain that the instruments consisted primarily of rods and lines of a primitive nature. Surveys were also of a crude sort. The location of the boundaries and the calculation of the areas of cheap land were not of great importance. In these surveys the measurements, in many cases, were dubious, as is seen from the frequent use of the terms "quae continet per aestimationem" (that [area] contained by estimation), and "quae continet per mensurationem" (that [area] contained by measurement), in designating litigation. Rights were frequently determined by the throw of a coin, while in other cases the boundaries ran "as far as a man could reach with his barge pole," so far "as the beech tree wherefrom the thief hung."[12]

Nevertheless the Saxons made two important contributions to land measuring. One, the open-field method of cultivation, indirectly affected surveying throughout Renaissance England and into the modern period. The second contribution,

[10] *Oxford English Dictionary* (Oxford, 1933). (Hereafter referred to as the *OED*).

[11] Nicholson, ref. 8, pp. 60–150.

[12] J. Stevenson, ed., *Chronicon Monasterii de Abington* (London, 1958), Vol. 1, pp. 56–59; W. H. Hart, ed., *Historia et Cartularium Monasterii Sancti Gloucestriae* (London, 1863–1867), Vol. 1, pp. 205–206.

the units of land measures, has directly influenced English land surveying to the present. These units of measure were not sanctioned by law until the twelfth century, when the English weights and measures were first sanctioned by statute.[13]

The Norman Conquest

After the Norman Conquest in 1066 it did not take William the Conqueror long to superimpose a more efficient administration of government on the existing government of the Saxons. William's strong authority gave the English feudal system more centralized control than its counterparts on the Continent; the tendency towards absolutism, implicit in William's rule, reached its culmination during the reign of Edward I (1272–1307).[14]

English history from 1300 to 1500 is marked by certain well-defined trends towards the beginning of a constitutional monarchy in place of Edward I's absolutism. During the thirteenth century we note the rise of the communities of merchants, merchant adventurers, and trading companies that were no longer dominated by foreigners but for the most part were composed of Englishmen.[15]

In the early part of the fourteenth century, the constitutional doctrine that all forms of direct taxation should receive the consent of the taxpayer was further developed. Richard II (1377–1399) attempted, somewhat unsuccessfully,

[13] B. Thorpe, *Ancient Laws and Institutions of England* (London, 1840), pp. 140–150; Darby Pickering, *The Statutes at Large* (Cambridge, 1762), Vol. 1, pp. 312–313.

[14] Helen Cam, *England Before Elizabeth* (London, 1950), pp. 79–113; George Clark, ed., *Oxford History of England* (Oxford, 1955).

[15] Cam, *op. cit.*, pp. 114–143; A. R. Myers, *England in the Late Middle Ages* (Hamondsworth, 1952), pp. 1–264.

to thwart the growing power and influence of the aristo-
crats. During his reign the Peasants' Revolt took place, at a
time when the monarchy was still suffering from the effects
of the Black Death and when the Hundred Years' War
added still more to the troubles of the government.

In the late fourteenth and early fifteenth centuries, the
process of the incorporation of the commons into the system
of the government was taking place. In this process the
rights and prerogatives of the common man were defined,
giving a greater voice to the rising middle class in the operation of the government. The second half of the fifteenth
century was taken up by the disastrous Wars of the Roses.
One result of these events was the breakdown of the medieval economy which led to the decay of feudalism, not only
as a social and political system but also as an economic system. Agriculture, which to a certain extent was overex-
panded during the fourteenth century, had had a period of
adjustment during the first half of the fifteenth century and
was now in a position to expand with the general economic
development of the country.

Agriculture and Land Tenure

From the Norman Conquest through the thirteenth century, agriculture was organized on the principle of graduated
independence and collective responsibility. In the early stages
of society the law, due to weakness, was unable to protect
the rights and property of the people. In consequence the
communities were grouped in small villages with the manor
house, church, and mill as the most conspicuous of the
whole group of houses.[16] The remaining buildings were

[16] Austin Poole, *Medieval England* (Oxford, 1958), Vol. 2, pp. 525–
600.

grouped in the village, and there were no detached farmhouses outside the village. This grouping of the communities gave a means of protection and at the same time made possible a continuous method of cultivation. In most cases during the twelfth and thirteenth centuries, the common rules of management kept the arable lands from deteriorating rapidly.

With the possible exception of a better utilization of animal power for farm work and transportation and widespread use of waterwheels, there was little improvement or technical advance in agriculture during this period. Possibly the greatest influence of the period on English agriculture came from the Cistercian movement in France. The only treatise in English on husbandry was that by Walter of Henley, written first in French with the title *Hosebondrie* about the middle of the thirteenth century and shortly thereafter translated into Latin and English.[17] The work remained the leading treatise on husbandry in English until the appearance of Sir Anthony Fitzherbert's *Husbandry* in 1523.

At the beginning of the Anglo-Norman period the arable lands were held in a compact unit under the direct supervivision of the lord of the manor, and his authority passed on down to the smallest land cultivator under his jurisdiction.[18] These landholdings passed from one tenant to another with little or no need for land surveys or resurveys, and, as a consequence, there was relatively little need for extensive land surveying. During the fourteenth and fifteenth centuries changes began to take place in agricultural landholdings throughout England. First was the beginning of the breakdown of feudalism, with the tight control of the arable

[17] Sarton, *Introduction*, Vol. 3, p. 497; Poole, *op. cit.*, p. 596.
[18] For a discussion of land tenure and enclosing consult Maurice Beresford, *The Lost Villages of England* (London, 1954); Roland E. Prothero, *English Farming Past and Present* (London, 1912); Howard L. Gray, *English Field Systems* (Cambridge, 1915).

lands in the manorial estates. Then there was an increase in the population and a steady growth of the country's economic development, bringing about a general rise in the economic status of the lower level of society. These factors led to a more diversified ownership of the arable lands, to an increase of enclosing, and to the reclamation of waste land.

Throughout the Anglo-Norman period the economic and intellectual status of the upper class of landholders generally improved. This improvement also extended to the middle-class inhabitants.

The Educational Movement

Although several sporadic educational movements had taken place in England before the Norman Conquest, the most important movement of this sort did not materialize until the twelfth century.[19] It is relatively certain that Oxford University had its beginning about 1170 but was not empowered with the right to confer the Master of Arts degree until 1258. Cambridge University was given the right to grant that degree in 1318.[20]

From their founding until the sixteenth century, the intellectual leaders of the country congregated at the two universities, and their contribution to the intellectual development of the country cannot be overestimated. For one thing these groups busied themselves with studies and translations of Greek and Arabic science. Interest in the study of astronomy and mathematics is noted, particularly trigonometry; the new Hindu-Arabic system of numbers had

[19] Poole, ref. 16, pp. 516–519; R. T. Gunther, *Early Science at Oxford* (Oxford, 1923), Vol. 2, pp. 1–76.
[20] S. C. Roberts, *British Universities* (London, 1947), pp. 1–13; Ernest Barker, *British Universities* (London, 1946), pp. 1–250.

been introduced into England, although their adoption and use were slow at this time.[21]

Many writers on arithmetic during the twelfth and thirteenth centuries were both abacist and algorithmist at the same time, but the importance of the introduction of the new system of writing numbers can scarcely be exaggerated. The efforts to establish experimental science were meager, but on the other hand, an approach to experimentation was demonstrated by Grosseteste (*ca.* 1175–1253) and by his pupil Roger Bacon (*ca.* 1214–1294). The last half of the twelfth century and the whole of the thirteenth century witnessed a renaissance of English philosophical and scientific studies.[22] During the thirteenth and fourteenth centuries there was also growth in technology, demanding new and better scientific instruments as well as a higher degree of accuracy in measurements.

Anglo-Norman Surveying

The technical development of Anglo-Norman surveying was not impressive; it differed little from that used by the Romans and Saxons many hundreds of years earlier. Probably the most important instrument that the medieval surveyor had in his possession was a measuring instrument of length, which no doubt was a rod or cord. In addition to the measuring instrument of length, the surveyor probably had some short rods or staves that he used to lay off straight distances or to mark corners or turning points. There was

[21] Sarton, *Introduction*, Vol. 2, pp. 740–755; A. von Braunmühl, *Vorlesungen über die Geschichte der Trigonometrie* (Leipzig, 1900), Vol. 1, pp. 108–109.

[22] Sarton, *Introduction*, Vol. 2, pp. 660–674, 714, 1054–1074; Poole, ref. 16, pp. 584–589; A. C. Crombie, *History of Science* (London, 1952), pp. 1–143; C. H. Haskins, *Studies in the History of Science* (Cambridge, 1924), pp. 9–40.

little need for angle-measuring instruments, since the surveyor paid little attention to angle measuring. Likewise we do not find any records where trigonometric methods were used in determining distances or angles; these were generally determined by similar triangles.

An important event in the development of surveying in England was the standardization of the measures used in the survey, which took place about 1277 in the reign of Edward I (1272–1307), when the first attempt was made to standardize all weights and measures.[23] Although rod-lengths from 12 to 24 feet were consistently used in England throughout the Anglo-Norman period, the length of the statute English rod was set at 16½ feet.[24] It is probable that this was the length of a North German land measure called the *ruthen*, which was brought to England by the Angles or Saxons. This measure was established as the English rod of 16 Rhineland feet, but at the time of the adoption of the statute rod it was adjusted to comply with the standard or King's foot; and, since 16 Rhineland feet were approximately 16.475 English feet, the German *ruthen* was slightly adjusted to correspond to 16½ English feet.[25] This length then became the statute English rod. There are numerous references in Middle English to a rod of 16 feet which in themselves would seem to support this hypothesis. At the same time the statute acre was set at 160 square rods, measured with the statute rod of 16½ feet.

Several primitive survey maps are to be found in medieval English literature. One is a survey map illustrating a

[23] Watson, ref. 8, pp. 50–110.

[24] Nicholson, ref. 8, pp. 30–118; Darby Pickering, *The Statutes at Large* (Cambridge, 1762), Vol. 1, pp. 312–313.

[25] Nicholson, ref. 8, pp. 60–150; H. W. Chisholm, *On the Science of Weighing and Measuring* (London, 1877); W. S. B. Woodhouse, *Measures, Weights, and Monies of All Nations* (London, 1890); A. E. Berryman, *Historical Metrology* (London, 1953).

boundary dispute to settle the rights of the baronies of Bollingbrooke, Horncastle, and Schrivelsby in reference to Wildmore Fen.[26] The description and map were taken from the Psalter belonging to Kirkstead Abbey, but now at Beaumont College, Old Windsor. This map was drawn about 1300, but the description of the inquest was given about 1150. It is probably the earliest example of an English survey map which has North at the top and which shows the different parts of the region with any degree of accuracy. A number of names given on the map (Fig. 4) can be located on the Ordinance Map, although there are a few that cannot be located at all.

Summary

In summarizing the development of land surveying from the Saxon invasion through the Norman Conquest to the close of the fifteenth century, we find it slow and unimpressive. However, many factors arose during this period that were to exert great influence on surveying during the Renaissance and early modern period. Important among these was the advance in learning in general and science in particular, especially mathematics. The introduction of the Hindu-Arabic system of writing numbers with its methods of calculation was an advance over prevailing methods. Trigonometry and geometry, although used but little at first, were subjects that would be readily applied to surveying in all its forms.[27] The increased interest of the Fellows

[26] Bernard Webb, "An Early Map and Description of the Inquest on Wildmore Fen in the Twelfth Century," *Lincoln Architectural and Archaeological Reports and Papers, 2* (1944), 141–156; Derek J. Price, "Medieval Land Surveying and Topographical Maps," *The Geographical Journal, 121* (1955), 1–10.

[27] E. G. R. Taylor, *The Mathematical Practitioners of Tudor and Stuart England* (Cambridge, 1954), pp. 7–15. (Hereafter referred to as *Mathematical Practitioners*.)

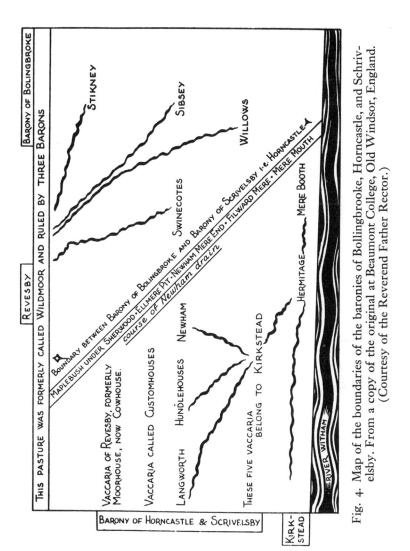

Fig. 4. Map of the boundaries of the baronies of Bollingbrooke, Horncastle, and Schriv-elsby. From a copy of the original at Beaumont College, Old Windsor, England. (Courtesy of the Reverend Father Rector.)

at Merton College, Oxford, in astronomy led to a desire for better instruments that would yield a higher degree of accuracy in measurements. Finally, the standardization of the units of land measures was an important step in the development of the methods of surveying.

By the close of the fifteenth century, the accumulated effects of these factors were having their effects on land surveying. Likewise, the rise in the general economic level of the country brought about an increase in the value of the arable land which, in turn, produced greater demands on the land surveyor.

The First Half of the Sixteenth Century

General Conditions

Modern English land surveying had its origins in the sixteenth century, partly brought about by the beginning of enclosing.[1] In its simplest form, enclosing was the process of combining the strips of the open fields into larger fields and then enclosing these larger fields with fences, hedges, or other boundaries. Later, meadows, parts of the commons, and reclaimed lands were brought into the enclosed system. This system of cultivation began in the late fifteenth century, gained momentum in the sixteenth century, and continued for many years thereafter. Combining and reorganizing the land of the open-field system to the enclosed form caused many complaints over titles, rights, and quantities of land involved and often led to a state of such complete confusion that the true issues were obscured before the courts. This

---

[1] H. C. Darby, "The Agrarian Contribution to Surveying in England," *The Geographical Journal, 82* (1933), 529–538; Roland E. Prothero, *English Farming Past and Present* (London, 1912), pp. 70–150.

confusion brought about a realization that a more exact determination of the quantities of land and a definite location of the boundaries were needed. Appeals were made to the surveyor for a correction of these faults.

In addition to the changes in land tenure and agriculture, there had been advances in instrument construction and use which were also applicable to surveying. Increase in navigation, for example, necessitated the use of some form of direction-finding instruments, usually the compass. The introduction of gunpowder brought progress in the military sciences, including the application of geometry to the problems of sighting and measuring angles in gunnery. Likewise, astronomy was making its demands for instruments of precision. These demands for better quality instruments with a relatively high degree of precision led to the development of a craft of mathematical instrument makers who later became world famous.

Although modern surveying originated in the sixteenth century, surveying then bore little general resemblance to modern methods. This was partially because of the problems peculiar to that age. Enclosure had involved countless changes in occupancy, and the court rolls are full of the records of the transfer of land by the customary tenants. The early surveys show the manors in every state of change from the open-field system of agriculture to the enclosed manor, while in many cases the commons and meadowlands were being enclosed.

Among the various manorial courts, still being held at this time, was the court of survey, presided over by a surveyor or by the steward of the manor. After the surveyor had made his perambulations over the manor, noting the buttes and bounds of the various holdings of the tenants, the bailiff summoned all the tenants to the court. Under oath they were required to give in detail all information regarding their holdings, crops, and any personal property. From this information the surveyor prepared an inventory of the manor, called the "court roll." This inventory gave the names of the tenants with their individual holdings, and the rents, fines, and services due the lord from each tenant and from each field in the manor. These court rolls or inventories were frequently elaborately written, often in Latin, with many decorations, embellishments, and a map or sketch of the manor.[2]

Sixteenth-Century Surveying Texts

Sixteenth-century surveying texts may be divided into two main groups: those concerned primarily with giving instruction to land stewards and overseers of the manor, and those concerned primarily with the measuring and the plotting of land. Typical of the first group are the texts by Fitzherbert (1523) and Barthelet (1545), while the second are typified by the texts of Benese (1537) and Cyprian Lucar (1590). Toward the close of the century some authors attempted to combine the two divisions into one text, best illustrated by the book of Valentine Leigh (1577).

Master Fitzherbert

The authorship of the first text on surveying printed in English, published at London in 1523, has long been in dispute. J. M. Riggs, in his article on Anthony Fitzherbert in the *Dictionary of National Biography*, and Walter W. Skeat in the introductory notes to his edition of *The Book*

[2] For a more complete discussion of the manorial courts and surveys see: Warren Ortman Ault, *Private Jurisdiction in England* (New Haven, 1923); H. S. Bennett, *Life on the English Manor* (New York, 1937); "English Manorial Documents," in Edward P. Cheyney, ed., *Translations and Reprints from the Original Sources of European History* (London, 1897), Vol. 3, No. 5; P. Vinogradoff, *The Growth of the Manor* (London, 1905).

of Husbandry, assign the authorship of the text on surveying and a text on husbandry definitely to Anthony Fitzherbert.[3] However, more recent research strongly indicates that Anthony's older brother John was more likely the author of both works. In an article in the *English Historical Review*, Reginald F. C. Fitzherbert points out that an examination of the two texts shows that the author was not a professional lawyer.[4] Somewhat later the investigations of Ernest Clark,[5] whose agricultural bibliography is unsurpassed, and Edwin Gay point out that the authorship of the books has always been doubtful. Gay states[6] that the facts in the case are few and that they have been poorly interpolated. His conclusions are the following:

1. The author of the book on surveying was also the author of the book on husbandry.
2. Thomas Barthelet, printer of the 1534 edition of the husbandry work, states that it was compiled by Master Fitzherbert.
3. The author of the book on husbandry states that he has had forty years' experience in agriculture.
4. In the 1534 edition of *Husbandry*, Barthelet refers to the author in the past tense, indicating that the author had died before this date.

[3] Anthony Fitzherbert, *The Book of Husbandry*, edited with introduction, notes, and glossary by the Rev. Walter W. Skeat (London, 1882).

[4] Reginald F. C. Fitzherbert, "The Authorship of the 'Book of Husbandry' and the 'Book of Surveying,'" *English Historical Review*, *12* (1897), 225–236.

[5] Ernest Clark, "Early Books on Agriculture," Discussion of the paper at February meeting, *Transactions of the Bibliographical Society*, *3* (1929), 160–162.

[6] Edwin F. Gay, "The Authorship of the Book of Husbandry and the Book of Surveying," *Quarterly Journal of Economics*, *18* (1904), 588–590.

Since Anthony Fitzherbert was born in 1470, it would hardly be possible for him to have forty years' experience in agriculture by 1523 when the text on surveying was written. The authorship is further complicated by Barthelet's reference to the author in the past tense, inasmuch as Anthony Fitzherbert did not die until 1538, whereas John Fitzherbert died in 1531.

The first edition, published in 1523, is listed in the *Short Title Catalogue*, number 11,005, with the title: *Here Begynneth a right Frutefull Mater: and hath to name the boke Surveynge and Improvementes*.[7] This edition consists of a title page and 63 folios, all printed in black letter. The book passed through seven editions in the sixteenth century, with one edition recorded by the British Museum in the seventeenth century. The original edition is addressed to the landed interest and is an explanation of the laws relating to manors. Fitzherbert sets forth the relation between the landlord and the tenant with observations on their respective moral rights and mutual obligations to each other. The author is also concerned with the best means of developing and improving an estate to the advantage of both the lord and the tenant. For the most part the text is based on the statute *Extenta Manerii*, once thought to be of the fourth year of the reign of Edward I (1276) but now classed as of uncertain date.

As defined by Fitzherbert, the duties and functions of the surveyor were many and varied. In the preface he states that the surveyor should prepare his findings in a small book or put them on a large piece of parchment. This parchment or book should show the "buttes" and "bounds" of all the

---

[7] Alfred W. Pollard and G. R. Redgrave, *A Short Title Catalogue of Books Printed in England, Scotland and Ireland and English Books Printed Abroad, 1475–1640* (London, 1926). (Hereafter referred to as the *Short Title Catalogue*.)

holdings as well as the leases, grants, and tenures. Along with this information he should state the number of buildings and their location and give a description of the lands, specifying whether they are meadow, grainland, or woodland, and by whom held. He should also record the value of all properties along with their rents and fines. The author then goes into considerable detail in giving the form for the preparation of this information.

During the first half of the sixteenth century the actual survey was what would be designated now as a chain survey; that is, surveying with a line-measuring instrument only. This type of surveying may have been executed with a line, cord, or rod, since there is no evidence that the chain, in the technical sense, was used by any surveyor before the seventeenth century. Master Fitzherbert gives us little information of the actual survey except to state that the furlongs and fields of all kinds should be bounded on all sides. The only mention of an angle-measuring instrument is a "dyall," which he states can be used on cloudy days to determine "which is East West North and South." This "dyall" may have been some form of pocket compass, or perhaps a small astrolabe with a compass inset on the backside.

The author states that the word "surveyor" is from the French, signifying an overseer, and that the surveyor must appraise and make recommendations to the lord of the manor. Although the author says that the surveyor should "butt" and "bound" all fields and properties, he gives no instructions for measuring the sides or angles of the fields, since the bearings of the sides are never given in the field notes. Likewise, he gives no rules for finding the areas of the various plats, and it is possible that the author expected the surveyor to estimate the areas of the fields by "viewing," that is, by going to a high place in the field and estimating the area by the eye. This method of determining the area of a parcel of land was used by many surveyors during the sixteenth and early seventeenth centuries. Furthermore, the author does not give any instructions for plotting the dimensions of the fields.

Richard Benese

The second book on surveying published in English was by Richard Benese (d. 1546), a canon of the Augustine priory of Merton in Surrey. He supplicated for the degree of Bachelor of Common Law at Oxford, 6 July 1619, and signed the surrender of the Augustine priory of Merton to Henry VIII on 16 April 1538. Before this he was a surveyor to Henry VIII, and it was during this period that he wrote his treatise on surveying. The treatise was prepared for the press by Thomas Paynell, also a canon of the priory of Merton, and the first edition of this work was printed by James Nicholson at Southwark, probably in 1537.[8]

The title page of the first edition reads as follows:

This boke/ sheweth the maner/ of measurynge of all ma/ ner of lande, as well as of/ woodlande, as of lande in the felde, and comptynge/ the true nombre of/ acres of the/ same. Newlye inuented and/ compyled by Sy: Ry/ charde Benese Cha/ non of Merton/ Abbay besyde/ London.

Printed in Southwarke in Saynt/ Thomas hospitall, by me James/ Nicholson.

---

[8] Benese's subsequent history is obscure. The name Benese is mentioned frequently as that of the holder of several beneficies and dignities, but whether they represent two or more persons is uncertain. John Aubrey states that "Tis Richard Benese was also the author of a little book, in 8vo . . .; quare Absolom Leech for it—tis about Physic." Joseph Foster, *Alumni Oxonienses* (London, 1891), Vol. 1. p. 110; *Fasti Ecclesiae Anglicanae* (Oxford, 1885), Vol. 1, p. 487; Vol. 2, p. 150; *Bibliotheca Britannico-Hibernica Thomas Tannero, Episcopo Asaphenesi* (London, 1748); John Aubrey, *Brief Lives* (Oxford, 1898); *State Papers of Henry VIII* (London, 1830), Vol. 1.

Although Fitzherbert's book was published almost fifteen years prior to Benese's, the later book represents the first real attempt to put into the hands of the surveyor or land measurer, as distinguished from the sixteenth-century manager of a manor, a simple, practical treatise on land surveying. The style is simple, and the explanations are clear and direct; the book gives every evidence of having been written by a person familiar with the practical art of land measuring.

The first edition (*Short Title Catalogue* number 1873) consists of a title page, three folios of preface, and 100 folios of text proper. The book is not divided into chapters, but each unnumbered section is headed with an appropriate title. The text as a whole is illustrated with forty-eight well-drawn and appropriate figures. In the first three folios, the author defines the units of line measures, stating that the standard foot should be the London standard of 12 inches. He then discusses the various perches used in measuring land; that is, the woodland perch of 18 feet and the field perch of $16\frac{1}{2}$ feet, or less.

Benese fixes the acre: "An acre bothe of woodlande, also of fylde lande is always .xl. perches in length, and .iiii. perches in bredth, although an acre of woodlande be more in quantity, than is an acre of fyldelande."[9] The author then describes the instruments which should be used in measuring the sides or boundaries of a piece of land. For this he suggests the one-perch, wooden rod as being satisfactory, but states that the cord or line of five perches in length is more convenient and measures much more rapidly than the rod. He cautions that the line should be treated with "whote waxe and rosyne" to prevent it from stretching and shrinking with the changes of the weather. Next Benese defines the parts of an acre in the following manner:

[9] Note the persistence of the idea of an area of land as a fixed length by a fixed breadth.

An acre conteyneth in it .viii^{xx}. perches.[10] An half acre conteyneth in it .iiii^{xx}. perches. The quarter of an acre (other wayes called a roode) conteyneth in it .xl. perches. An acre conteyneth in it .xl. dayworkes. A dayworke conteyneth in it .iiii. perches.

After the units of length and land measures have been defined and discussed, the author gives methods of finding the areas of certain simple geometrical figures, principally triangles, rectangles, trapeziums, and circles. Benese does not give a general method of finding the area of any of these but discusses each type of figure as a special case. In the illustrative examples, particularly when the altitude of the triangle is given in fractional form, the author is not very careful of the accuracy of the computed values; in most cases fractions are disregarded, although the error in the computed values may range from five to ten per cent of the true value. Apparently Benese realized the lack of computational skill on the part of most of his readers; to meet this difficulty he prepared four sets of tables—to be discussed later—to aid in the determination of the areas of figures and also in laying out parcels of land of different sizes and shapes.

The method of surveying which Benese outlines is the typical chain surveying of the sixteenth century, since he uses only the rod and line in his measurements. His first instruction is that the surveyor should "view" or go around the piece of land once or twice before the survey is made so that he can decide exactly how he will execute the survey. At this point he must decide whether he will measure the piece of ground as four sides or with more than four sides; that is, before the survey begins, he must decide whether or not the tract of ground is rectangular. The author suggests that when the plot is irregular the survey be made by divid-

---

[10] Multiples of twenty are written throughout the text in a similar manner; for example, viii^{xx} = 8(10 + 10) = 160. Multiples of 100 are written similarly; for example, 300 = iii^{c}. Folio A₃.

ing the tract of land up into a number of smaller parts. It is assumed that the surveyor will keep some record of the shape and dimensions of the parts into which the whole is divided. Benese proposes that this record be kept on a sheet of paper or by cutting notches on a stick (apparently the field notebook had not been developed).

He then discusses several unusual cases of survey. The first is where one side of the parcel of land borders on a stream. Benese recommends that a line be measured that will divide this irregular piece of land so that as much will be on one side as on the other side. The second case concerns hills and valleys whose superficial areas are to be computed rather than the plane area. In these cases two or three measurements are taken around the side of the hill or valley; then a straight line is run from the foot of the hill to its top or from the top of the valley to its bottom.

The text gives no method for obtaining the direction of the sides of the figures in the survey of a piece of land; Benese does not mention any instrument for determining the direction of the meridian or any other line in the survey. The discussion of the measurements of the sides is completed in about three pages of text.

Introducing his discussion of the computation of land areas, the author considers the areas of various geometrical figures, presumably taken from some edition of Euclid's works. These figures include different types of triangles, quadrilaterals (some of which are divided into triangles), polygons, and finally, circular figures. Benese then points out some of the errors that surveyors frequently make in computing the areas of irregular figures, in particular those figures which are four-sided but not rectangular. Figures of this type should be divided into a number of triangles, he suggests; then the area of each triangle is computed, and the total area of the irregular figure is found by adding the separate areas. The superficial area of a hillside or valley, instead of the plane areas enclosed by the boundaries, is computed by using the average of the three circumferences measured at the foot, middle, and crest of the hill or valley multiplied by the slant height. In nearly every case the method of finding the area, if rectangular, is to multiply the length by the width. If triangular, the area is found by taking one half the product of the base by the altitude. The author also discusses the areas of a number of figures which would seldom or never occur in actual practice; for example, areas whose boundaries were circular or polygonal in shape.

In order to facilitate the computation of the areas of various figures, Benese states:

For lykewyse as a marke[11] of money conteyneth in it .viii^{xx}. pence, so dothe an acre conteyne in it .viii^{xx}. perches. And lyke-wyse as a marke of money doth conteyne in it .xl. grotes, so doth an acre conteyne in it .xl. dayworkes. And as a grote dothe conteyne in it .iiii. pêce, so doth a dayworke conteyne in it .iiii. perches.

In the table following these definitions, the number of square perches is given on the left in terms of pence, shillings, and pounds, whereas the area is given on the right in terms of the land units of square perches, dayswork, roods, and acres.

Although this table was constructed to aid those with little or no ability in calculations, the author still fears that many will not be able to use the table. Benese therefore gives a second table for the calculation of areas: this is a two-way

[11] The mark or marc is from the Anglo-Saxon *marc*, which was probably related to the German *mark* and Icelandic *mork*. This coin was probably current during the late Saxon and Middle English periods and was equal to 13 shillings and 4 pence or 160 pence. Since the English pound was a denomination of money equivalent to 20 shillings, or 240 pence, and the pound was also equivalent to 1½ marks, and since the mark, in terms of square perches, represented an acre, then the pound, in terms of square perches, would represent 1½ acres.

table giving the area for a known length and breadth in acres, roods, dayswork, and square perches for values of length from 1 to 120 perches and for values of breadth from 1 to 120 perches. One example from this table (Fig. 5) shows the cell for a length of 67 perches and a breadth of 7 perches,

which is read as follows: 2 acres, 3 roods, 7 dayswork, and 1 square perch. Two other tables are given in the text: the first is used in dividing a plot of land into a given number of rectangular strips with a given area; the final table is to aid in computing the value of a given area of ground when the price per acre is given.

Benese gives no instructions for plotting the bounds of the different tracts of land, nor is there any indication from the text that a plat or map of land is to be made. Likewise he makes no mention of a report to the lord of the manor, such as that suggested by Fitzherbert.

The text apparently passed through four editions or printings during the next thirty years, with succeeding editions in 1539, 1562, and 1564. These editions differ but little, except that one or more of the tables were omitted in some printings. In the second edition, printed in 1539, the seventy-five pages of tables are completely omitted, but in other respects the edition is identical with the first.

The two publications of Fitzherbert and Benese with their later editions were the only texts on surveying published during the first half of the sixteenth century. There is, it is true, one more title: *Here beginneth a ryght fruteful mater*.

The lengthe.

The bredthe.

	61	62	63	64	65	66	67	68	69	70
1	1 5. 1	1 5. 2	1 5. 3	1 6	1 6. 1	1 6. 2	1 6. 3	1 7	1 7. 1	1 7. 2
2	3 2 1	3 1. 2	3 2	3 2. 2	3 3	3 3. 2	3 4	3 4. 2	3 5	3
3	1 5. 3	1 6. 2	1 7. 1	1 8	1 8. 3	1 9. 2	1 1 1 1	1 1 1. 3	1 2. 2	1
4	1 2 1 2	1 2 1 3	1 2 1 4	1 2 1 5	1 2 1 6	1 2 1. 2 7	1 2 1. 2 8	1 2 1. 2 9	1 2 1. 3	
5	1. 3 6. 1	1. 3 7. 2	1. 3 8	3 2 3	2 1. 1	2. 2. 2 3.	2 3. 3 5	2 6. 1	2 7 2	
6	2. 1 1. 2	2 1. 3	1. 1 4. 2	2. 1 6	2. 1 7. 2	2. 1 9	2. 1 2 2	2. 2 3. 2	2. 2 5.	2. 2
7	2. 2 6. 3	2. 2 8. 2	2. 3 1	2 2	2. 3 3.	2. 3 3. 2	2 7. 1	3 9	2. 3 3	3 3 2. 2
8	3 2	3 4	3 6	3 8	3. 1 3. 1 2	3. 1 4	3. 1 6	3. 1 8	3. 1	3. 2
9	3. 1 7. 1	3. 1 9. 2	3. 2 1. 3	3. 2 4	3. 2 6. 1	3. 2 8. 2	3 3 3 3	3 5. 1	3 7. 2	3
10	3. 3 2. 2	3. 3 5	3. 3 7. 2	4	4 2. 2	4 5	4 7. 2	4. 1	4. 1 2. 2	4. 1 5

The fyrst parte.

Fig. 5. A page from Benese's table of areas. From a copy of
Benese's This boke / sheweth the maner / of measurynge
of all ma / ner of lande.
(Courtesy of the Henry Huntington Library.)

& hathe to name the boke of Surveyinge and Improuementes,
by Thomas Barthelet, published in 1545.[12] The British
Museum Catalogue and the Short Title Catalogue both give
Thomas Barthelet as the author; however, the text apparently
is nothing more than an edition of Fitzherbert's book, which
was probably edited by Barthelet before it was published.
The text of this book is almost identical with the text of the
first three editions of Fitzherbert's work. Since John Fitz-

[12] From a microfilm copy of an original copy owned by the British
Museum, from whom permission for its use has been obtained.

herbert died in 1531, it is more than likely that Thomas Barthelet made some changes in the title page, added some comments in the prologue, and saw that the book was printed.

Summary

Surveying developments during the first half of the sixteenth century were few. As far as can be determined, little or nothing was accomplished in instrument construction. However, the two texts on surveying by Fitzherbert and Benese were major contributions, and their influence extended throughout the sixteenth century.

The Second Half of the Sixteenth Century

General Conditions

Formal instruction in science and the art of surveying barely existed at the beginning of the second half of the sixteenth century. Surveying textbooks were virtually non-existent, for the first text on surveying was not written until the second quarter of the century. Not only were textbooks lacking, but suitable books on arithmetic and geometry were difficult to obtain.[1]

One of the first educators to recognize the needs of the scientific profession in England was Leonard Digges,[2] who

[1] The first arithmetic printed in English, *An Introduction for to Lerne to Recken with the Pen or with the Counters*, was published anonymously in 1537. A. W. Richeson, "The First Arithmetic Printed in English," *Isis*, 37 (1947), 47-56.

[2] Leonard Digges (1510-1550) was a mathematician of ability and a notable writer on applied mathematics and military subjects. Several of his works were left in manuscript form at his death, but were later published by his son, Thomas. David Eugene Smith, *History of Mathematics* (Boston, 1923-1925); Francis Johnson, "Letter to the Editor," *The Times Literary Supplement* (London, 5 April 1934); Louise Diehl Patterson, "Leonard and Thomas Digges. Biographical

played an important part in the development of methods for artisans and surveyors by writing the *Tectonicon* and *Pantometria*. The *Tectonicon* attempted to give a simple treatment for the construction and use of instruments for the average surveyor and artisan. On the other hand, the *Pantometria*, written by Leonard Digges but published by his son Thomas,[3] was intended to teach the correct geometrical principles of surveying and mensuration. In addition to the work of Leonard and Thomas Digges there were two other writers, John Dee and Robert Recorde,[4] who were pioneers in writing textbooks and translating texts from other languages into English.

These early English writers and translators seem to have taken pride in preparing books on mathematics and other scientific subjects that could be successfully used by the practical man. They borrowed and built up a technical vocabulary and a technique that were clear and simple. The average sixteenth-century reader was not capable of under-

---

Notes," *Isis*, *42* (1952), 120–121; Taylor, *Mathematical Practitioners*, p. 75.

[3] Thomas Digges (1546–1595), the son of Leonard Digges, was a pupil and friend of John Dee. He was frequently named with Dee and Thomas Herriot as one of the three leading mathematicians of his day. Thomas published several works of his own and edited and published the *Pantometria* of his father. *Dictionary of National Biography* (Oxford, 1885–1939). (Hereafter referred to as the *DNB*.) R. T. Gunther, *Early Science in Cambridge* (Oxford, 1937), p. 32; Taylor, *loc. cit.*; Johnson, *loc. cit.*; Patterson, *loc. cit.*

[4] John Dee (1527–1608) studied at St. John's College, Cambridge, where he took his A.B. degree in 1546. Dee probably exerted a greater influence on sixteenth century scientist than any other Englishman of the century. Smith, *History*, Vol. 1, pp. 323–324; Taylor, *Mathematical Practitioners*, p. 170. Robert Recorde (*ca.* 1510–1558) was educated at Oxford and Cambridge. Recorde is frequently referred to as the founder of English mathematics, since he wrote in English and offered an unique originality in presenting his subject. He became one of the most influential mathematical writers of the sixteenth century. Smith, *History*, Vol. 1, 318–320; Taylor, *Mathematical Practitioners*, p. 167.

standing much of the scientific writings of the times; as a result, a number of popular scientific writings were published for him.[5]

Evidence of the training, preparation, and instruction given the average artisan and surveyor is furnished by many sources. Foster Watson states[6] that the education of the lower classes was usually of an apprentice nature, and in consequence they were taught little or no mathematics or science. It had taken generations to build up the classico-religious tradition in education, and there was great resistance to changing this curriculum. For the most part the quadrivium of arithmetic (theoretical), geometry, astronomy, and music was taught to the nobility and the upper classes. Before Robert Recorde very little arithmetic, ciphering, was taught, and the study of this type of arithmetic was almost completely outside the academic system.[7]

This lack of training in mathematics exerted a considerable influence on the construction of early surveying instruments. As Taylor points out, deficiencies in mathematical training were no doubt an important factor in the designing of the plane table. This instrument provided the practitioner who was not adept at calculations with an instrument that would perform more or less mechanically the many arithmetical calculations in land measuring. Lack of mathematical ability on the part of the surveyors played an important role in the construction of instruments with scales and indices to assist in determining inaccessible heights and distances. These scales were in almost constant use until trigonometry came into use late in the first half of the eighteenth century.[8]

[5] Francis R. Johnson, *Astronomical Thought in Renaissance England* (Baltimore, 1937), pp. 10–97.

[6] Foster Watson, *The Beginning of the Teaching of Modern Subjects in England* (London, 1909).

[7] Watson, *op. cit.*, pp. 213–214.

[8] Watson, *op. cit.*, pp. 288–332.

If the conditions for the study of arithmetic were bad, those for the study of elementary geometry were perhaps even worse. The first English book concerned completely with geometry did not appear until 1557, and the first English translation of Euclid's *Elements* from the Greek was not published until some thirteen years later. At the universities the study of geometry was almost nonexistent during the first half of the century, and the subject was only halfheartedly taught in the second half. The average engineer and surveyor not only lacked the fundamental principles of geometry, but his computational skill was so poor that he was unable to make use of the little geometrical knowledge he did possess.

Many of the errors of the early surveyors were probably due to ignorance of the fundamental principles of geometry. One of the earliest surveyors to point out this deficiency was Edward Worsop, a London surveyor, who states that the mathematical training of most surveyors was so inadequate that many of them ignored fractions completely. He says that every surveyor should be able to prove his work by geometry; further,

. . . euen so ought he, to be accounted insufficient for a land measurer, ye hath not red Euclides Elementes, but is ignorant of his definitions and propositions; especially such as concerne liniare & superficial measures. As Euclide is a Greek author, so is the name of his Elements greeke to a great number of such landemeaters, as holde their credit, by the sign of the instrument.[9]

The quality of instruction in mathematics and the allied sciences had a marked effect on surveying texts as well as on the actual work done by surveyors of the sixteenth, seventeenth, and eighteenth centuries. In practically every text on surveying written before the beginning of the eighteenth

[9] Edward Worsop, *A Discoverie of Sundrie Errours and Faults Daily Committed by Landemeaters* (London, 1582), Folios E_3 and F_1.

century, from 50 to 100 pages were devoted to arithmetic and geometry. Many short cuts, aids, and tables were included in these early texts. One of the most interesting of them, formulated by Richard Benese and used by several other writers of the sixteenth century, was a table for the calculation of areas by a comparison with the units of money (see Chapter Three). Likewise, tables were frequently given for the number of acres and fractional parts of an acre for plots of land with different lengths and widths.

In order to overcome the lack of mathematical and scientific training, a number of men during the second half of the sixteenth century attempted to bring to the surveyor, navigator, engineer, and artisan a description of the existing instruments and a simple discussion of the mathematics required to use them. Some of these men have been mentioned above in the discussion of the conditions of the schools. Earlier in the century Robert Recorde had published his important work on arithmetic; later Sir Henry Billingsly, probably with the help of John Dee, had translated Euclid's *Elements* from the Greek into English; and William Bedwell had translated Ramus' *French Geometry* into English. Notable in the practical application of mathematics were William Cunningham, William Bourne, and Leonard Digges.

In 1559 William Cunningham[10] published in London his *Cosmographicall Glasse*, one of the first English works on cosmography. In this book Cunningham gives various diagrams of quadrants and other surveying and astronomical instruments, among them a circular plate divided into thirty-two parts with an alidade attached at the center and an eccentrically located compass needle. No degrees are given

---

[10] William Cunningham (1531–1586) was educated at Cambridge and Heidelberg Universities. He is known to have surveyed and mapped Norwich, his birthplace, and to have constructed a new type quadrant and an astronomer's dial. In later life Cunningham practiced medicine in London. Taylor, *Mathematical Practitioners*, p. 172.

on the large circular plate or on the compass inset, as can be seen from the diagram (Fig. 6). The similarity of the discussion of these instruments and the problems on triangulation in Cunningham's and Bourne's works suggests either that Bourne had used Cunningham's work in the preparation of his manuscript or that they both had drawn from the same sources, which must have been Gemma Frisius and Tartaglia.

Another prominent writer of this period was William Bourne,[11] one of the first Englishmen to write in the vein

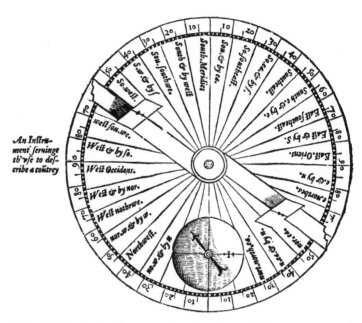

Fig. 6. Cunningham's surveying instrument. From a copy of Cunningham's *Cosmographicall Glasses*.
(Courtesy of the Folger Shakespeare Library.)

[11] E. G. R. Taylor, *Tudor Geography 1485–1583* (London, 1930); and E. G. R. Taylor, "William Bourne: A Chapter in Tudor Geography," *The Geographical Journal*, 72 (1928), 329–341.

of popular science. He was at one time an innkeeper and had served as a gunner and portreeve in the town of Gravesend. A keen student, particularly of mathematics, and a very practical man, Bourne desired to translate into use whatever he read, whether in English or a foreign language; that is, to put into simple language the works of others so that practical men could use them. The influence of Continental writers, noticeable in Bourne, led to significant developments in many phases of navigation and surveying. The manuscript of one of his important works written about 1572 is now in the British Museum. The first part of this manuscript is on gunnery and range finding, obviously based on Tartaglia's *Quesiti et Inventioni*, and the second part deals with the measurements of heights and distances by using the reverse side of the astrolabe. Bourne discusses triangulation with methods similar to those outlined by Gemma Frisius, and he gives the construction of maps following the methods of Apian in the *Cosmographia*.

The surveying instrument proposed by Bourne is an improvement over those suggested by Gemma Frisius and Tartaglia, and, as stated by Taylor,[12] it is less clumsy than the astrolabe with the compass inset which had to be held in a horizontal position when used. This instrument (Fig. 7) consisted of a circular brass plate graduated along the outer edge in degrees, with 0° at the west end of the east-west meridian line and continuing clockwise to 360°. Radiating from the center were the thirty-two point lines of the compass rose, and attachèd to the center points was the "athelidey" (alidade) with sights attached to its ends. A compass needle inset was attached on the north-south line between the center and the north end of the line. No mention is made of a tripod or staff on which to place the instrument, and

[12] E. G. R. Taylor, "William Bourne: A Chapter in Tudor Geography," *The Geographical Journal*, 72 (1928), 336–337.

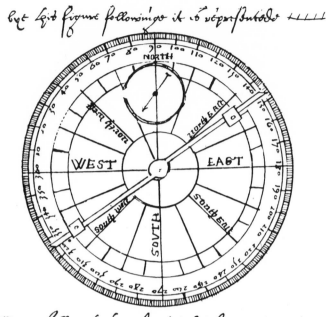

Fig. 7. Surveying instrument of William Bourne. From the
Sloane ms. no. 3651 in the British Museum.
(Courtesy of the Director.)

we may thus infer that Bourne used a tree stump or other
flat object.

The important contribution of Bourne's manuscript to
surveying is its illustrated example of surveying by triangulation, which was apparently carried out by his surveying
instrument. The map of this survey is drawn to a scale of
1/52,800, and Fig. 8 shows a portion of this work. In the
manuscript Bourne explains how to make a topographical
survey of a river, its banks and surrounding country, by

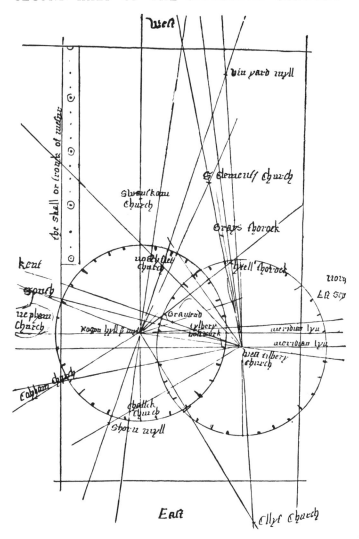

Fig. 8. A triangulation problem of William Bourne. From the
Sloane ms. no. 3651 in the British Museum.
(Courtesy of the Director.)

means of an operator in a boat with a compass for fixing the bearings of points on the banks of the river and objects some distance from the river. At the end of the survey he takes the bearings of two objects already located by the triangulation of the surrounding country. Although some form of the surveyor's chain was already known at this time, Bourne resorts to pacing to establish the length of his base line for the triangulation. In 1578 Bourne published *A Book Called the Treasure for Travellers* containing an account of the problem of triangulation, which had previously been given in manuscript form, as well as other instructions to surveyors.[13] However, this work does not contain that portion of the manuscript devoted to topographical surveying.

The third writer of the period, and one who possibly contributed more to English surveying and engineering than any other sixteenth century writer, was the well-known Leonard Digges. Not only was he a first-rate mathematician but he was also a writer of importance on practical scientific subjects. His purpose in writing was to convey to the surveyor, the artificer, or the stone mason the necessary mathematics and scientific principles in a form that could be easily understood and put into practice.

Leonard Digges and His Instruments

Although Leonard Digges attended University College, Oxford, and was one of the outstanding technical writers of the second half of the sixteenth century, he seems to have had slight contact with Continental scientists. He did, however, have indirect contact through the eminent scientist and mathematician John Dee (1527–1608). After receiving his A.B. degree from Cambridge, Dee had traveled extensively

[13] William Bourne, *A Book Called the Treasure for Travellers* (London, 1578).

over the Continent, studying for two years at the University
of Louvain. Here he was a student of Gemma Frisius and
Orontius Fine and had frequent contacts with Mercator, the
great cartographer. These four men were lifelong friends.
On one of his trips to the Continent, Dee procured the most
important works of Apian, Fine, and Mercator,[14] all of which
he subsequently installed in his library at Mortlake on the
Thames. It is here, no doubt, that Leonard Digges met John
Dee and gained access to the foreign writings as well as
much firsthand information from Dee himself.

Digges' first effort to provide a practical treatise for the
land surveyor is found in a book published in London in
1556 with the title *A Booke Named Tectonicon*. The first
five chapters give simple rules and methods for the use and
application of arithmetic and geometry to the measuring
of the areas of simple geometric figures; the remaining six-
teen chapters, including the appendix, are primarily an application of the principles outlined in the first five chapters,
along with the use and application of the various instruments
at the command of the land measurer, carpenter, and artisan.
It seems quite evident from the preface that the sole aim of
Digges in preparing this book was to give the reader a simple
and straightforward handbook and reference guide.

Aside from the general rules of areas, the text provides
little information for the land surveyor, except a guide for
the construction and use of three instruments for determining distances. These instruments are the geometrical
square on the side of a ruler, the carpenter's square, and the
cross-staff, which Digges calls the "profitable staff." In his
discussion of land measurements Digges mentions two other

---

[14] Gerardus Mercator (1512–1594), the Flemish mathematician and
geographer, was born at Rupelmonde, Flanders, and studied at Bois-
le-Duc and the University of Louvain, where he was closely associated
with Gemma Frisius. Smith, *History*, Vol. 1, 234.

instruments, the pole and cord for measuring distances, but does not mention any instrument for measuring direction. The construction of the square on the carpenter's rule (Fig. 9) is interesting in its simplicity: two sights are placed on one edge of the rule near the ends, while on one side of the rule and in the center of its length a geometrical square is constructed. The two sides of this square are divided into 10, 12, 60, or 100 parts, and inscribed within it is the quadrant of a circle divided into degrees; that is, from 0 to 90°. At the center of the arc of this circle is attached a cord with a plummet at the end. This instrument was used almost exclusively for leveling and determining heights and altitudes. Digges was apparently familiar with the geometrical square and quadrant which were used extensively on the Continent, and it is probable that Digges used Apian's *Instrument-Buch*[15] as a source for much of the material in the *Tectonicon.*

In order to determine horizontal distances, Digges makes use of the carpenter's square. In Fig. 10 he shows that if one places the right angle of the square on a staff, which has been divided into 100 or 1,000 parts, and then sights the distant object along the long side of the square and measures the base of the smaller triangle, one will then be able by means of similar triangles to obtain the unknown side or distance.[16]

A third instrument which Digges prized very highly, also described in the *Tectonicon,* is referred to as the "Instrument Geometricall," or the "profitable staffe." In his enthusiasm for this instrument, Digges states:

I said in the beginning that no little booke would containe the making and manifold fruites of this princely instrument, if it were set forth as it ought to be in his perfection. Certes the

---

[15] Peter Apian, *Instrument-Buch* (Ingolstadt, 1533).
[16] Leonard Digges, *A Book Named Tectonicon* (London, 1556), Folio F. (Hereafter referred to as *Tectonicon.*)

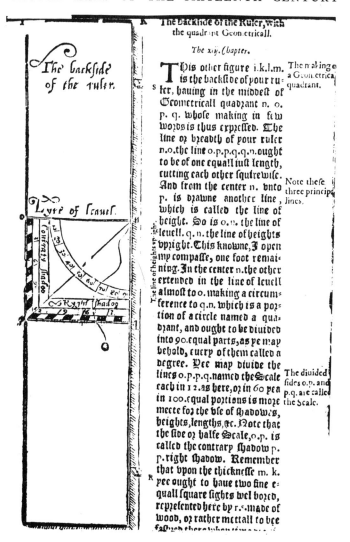

The backfide of the Ruler, with the quadrant Geometricall.

The xij. Chapter.

THis other figure i.k.l.m. is the backfide of your ruler, hauing in the middeſt of Geometricall quadjant n. o. p. q. whofe making in few wozds is thus expreſſed. The line oz bzeadth of your ruler n.o.the line o.p.p.q.q.n.ought to be of one equall iuſt length, cutting each other ſquirewiſe. And from the center n. vnto p. is dzawne another line, which is called the line of height. So is o.n. the line of leuell. q. n. the line of heights vpright. This knowne, I open my compaſſe, one foot remaining. In the center n. the other extended in the line of leuell almoſt too. making a circumference to q.n. which is a poztion of a circle named a quadjant, and ought to be diuided into 90. equall parts, as ye may behold, euery of them called a degree. Yee may diuide the lines o.p.p.q.named the Scale each in 12. as here, oz in 60 pea in 100. equall poztions is moze meete foz the vſe of ſhadowes, heights, lengths, &c. Note that the ſide oz halfe Scale, o.p. is called the contrary ſhadow p. p. right ſhadow. Remember that vpon the thickneſſe m. k. yee ought to haue two fine equall ſquare ſights wel bozed, repzeſented here by r.s. made of wood, oz rather mettall to bee

The making of a Geometricall quadrant.

Note theſe three principall lines.

The diuided ſides o.p. and p.q. are called the Scale.

Fig. 9. Digges' use of the carpenter's rule with the geometrical square. From Digges' *Tectonicon*.
(Courtesy of the Library of Congress.)

55

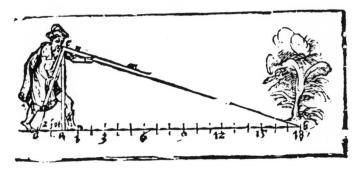

Fig. 10. Digges' use of the carpenter's square in measuring distances. From Digges' *Tectonicon*.
(Courtesy of the Library of Congress.)

even here maketh me confess the same: yea, that there is no instrument so general and profitably pleasant.[17]

The construction of this instrument (Fig. 11) is as follows: two small straight rods of wood or metal, about 5 feet long, are prepared and each foot length of the rods is divided into 12 equal parts. The two rods are so prepared and divided that they may be fitted together, end to end, to form a rod 10 feet long. In addition to these two pieces, four short pieces (3, 6, 12, and 24 inches long, respectively) are also constructed. Each of these short pieces has a hole of sufficient size mortised in the center so that the piece will slide easily along the 10-foot rod. These short pieces are called the crossbars and are used two at a time in such lengths as are needed (Fig. 12). Although this form of the cross-staff is slightly different from that shown by Apian in his *Instrument-Buch*, Digges' is no doubt a modification of it.[18]

In 1571 the last publication of Leonard Digges appeared in London with the title *A Geometrical Treatise Named*

[17] Digges, *op. cit.*, Folios G_1^v to H_1^v.
[18] Apian, *Instrument-Buch*, Folios N_1^v to N_4^r; and Digges, *Tectonicon*, Folio G_1^v.

The making of this profitable
Rodde or Staffe.

YE shall prepare two small, streight, stiffe, round, or rather square rods of mettall or of wood, well plained of like bignesse and length. Although it make no matter of what length, yet to auoide the errours, which little instruments, and short staues bring, and also to beare with the rude vnwonted handling of such Artificers: let our Rods bee each fiue, or at the least three foote, and euery foote diuided in 12. euen parts or Inches, as yee see a.b. and c.d. These Rods must bee forged with a voyce in the end of them to ioyne readily tenne or sixe foote in length, (when time requireth) as the figure e. f. sheweth. Also yee must get (by the helpe of some Craftsman) foure other like Rods, the longer g. 2. foote: the next h. 1. foote: the other 1.6. Inches, then k. 3. Inches, the last and shortest l. 1. Inch, and ½. Each of these must haue in their middest a hole, that the long staffe of ten foote may bee put through them, and they moued on him at pleasure vp and downe, alwayes cutting the longer staffe c. f. Squirewise, and made to tarry on any diuision, as

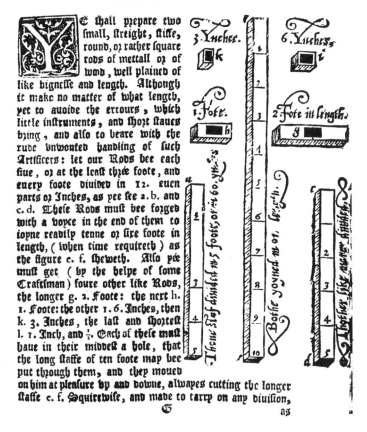

Fig. 11. The unassembled parts of the profitable or cross-staff. From Digges' *Tectonicon.* (Courtesy of the Library of Congress.)

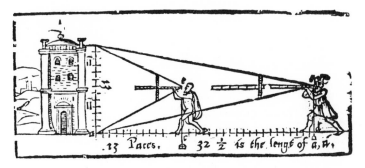

Fig. 12. Finding an inaccessible height with the profitable or cross-staff. From Digges' *Tectonicon.*
(Courtesy of the Library of Congress.)

Pantometria. Both the first and second editions were edited and published by the author's son, Thomas Digges. Although many writers of the late seventeenth and early eighteenth centuries felt that Digges' books were too highly specialized for the average practicing surveyor, his second book is important if for no other reason than that it is the first text in English to give a description of the theodelitus and the topographical instrument.

The first section of the book, called "Longimetria," is the most important from the standpoint of the surveyor. Here the author discusses the measurements of distances with the surveying instruments used for this purpose and the construction of the theodelitus[19] and the "instrument topo-

[19] This term is spelled "theodelitus" and "theodolite" in the *Pantometria.* The origin of the word with Digges is uncertain. R. T. Gunther in his *Early Science in Oxford* (p. 365) has suggested that theodolite or theodelite was a corruption of *althelida,* which was in turn a corruption of the Arabic *alhidada,* an index. W. W. Skeat and Ernest Weekley, in their *Etmylogical Dictionaries of the English Language,* are of the opinion that Digges took the word from the Old French, *Theodolet,* the name of a poem translated from the late Latin *Theodulus.* Skeat, however, is more inclined to believe that it

graphicall." Other than the two instruments last named and the geometrical square, those used by Digges are almost identical with those previously discussed in the *Tectonicon*. However, Digges' instructions for the construction of the geometrical square (Fig. 13), differ somewhat from those

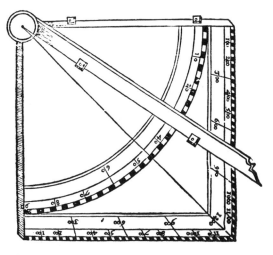

Fig. 13. A geometrical square by Digges. From Digges' *Panto-metria*.
(Courtesy of the Library of Congress.)

is a reference to a mathematician named Theodulus. A search does not indicate any Greek mathematician of importance by this name. A note following the definition of theodolite in the *OED* states that theodelite is the vernacular form of the Latinized *theodolitus,* which subsequently became *theodolite* in English. The word was not known in French or German before the nineteenth century. An examination of the works of Leonard and Thomas Digges, by whom the word was first used, fails to give any clue of its meaning. The *OED* does not believe it is in any way related to *alhidada* but suggests that the word has the look of being derived from the Greek. This source further suggests that it may be an unscholarly formation, like many modern names of inventions, from θεωαι, I view, or θεω, behold, and ἠλ·os, visible, clear, manifest with a meaningless termination.

in his *Tectonicon*. A square whose sides are about 18 inches in length is constructed on a smooth plate of metal or on a wooden board; then on two adjacent sides of this square a scale of 1,200 parts is divided, and within the square there is constructed the quadrant of a circle which is divided into degrees. An index is then constructed with two sights: the one made of a thin metal plate about 3 inches tall with a small slit extending almost to the top; the other sight, somewhat shorter than the first, is made with a pin placed in the center of the upper edge so that the head of the pin could be sighted on a distant object through the slit in the other sight. The index is joined to the square at the corner diagonally opposite the corner where the two scales meet.[20] After giving several examples for the use of the geometrical square the author continues with the construction of the theodelitus.

The theodelitus consists of a circle of radius of 1 foot or more drawn upon a metal plate, the circle being divided into 360 parts or degrees. These divisions were usually subdivided into six parts or divisions of 10 minutes each. Within two adjacent quadrants of the circle there were constructed two geometrical squares, whose sides were divided into twelve equal parts. The index and sights of this instrument were similar to those used on the geometrical square, except that the index was attached at its center to the center of the circle, as shown in Fig. 14. The backside of the instrument was made smooth so that it could be used as a flat surface upon which to plot the field notes. Following the description of the construction of the instrument is an example showing the use of the instrument in determining the distance between two inaccessible points by means of two stations and

[20] Leonard Digges, *A Geometrical Treatise Named Pantometria* (London, 1571) Chap. 22, Folio C$_3^r$.

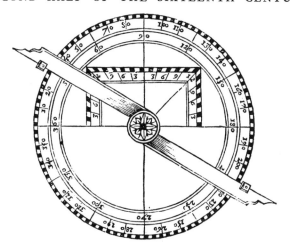

Fig. 14. The theodelitus. From Digges' *Pantometria*.
(Courtesy of the Library of Congress.)

a simple form of triangulation.[21] After giving these instructions Digges proceeds with the construction of another instrument.

Construction of the topographical instrument involved combining the theodelitus (Fig. 14) within the geometrical square to form the horizontal limb of the instrument (Fig. 15). The two adjoining sides of the geometrical square were divided into at least 1,200 parts, and a hole was drilled into the plate at the point of the intersection of the diagonals of the square (Point *A*, Fig. 15). This point was the center of the circle of the theodelitus and also the point of attachment of the sights of the theodelitus to the instrument.

In addition to this combination there was constructed a semicircle, divided into 180 parts or degrees, and within the

---

[21] Digges, *op. cit.*, Chap. 27, Folios F$_2^v$.

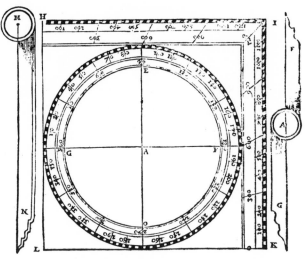

Fig. 15. The topographical instrument. From Digges' *Panto-metria*.
(Courtesy of the Library of Congress.)

semicircle were also constructed two small geometrical squares (Fig. 16). Attached to the semicircle was a support with a pointed end of such size that it could be placed and turned in the hole, *A*, at the center of the circle and sights of the theodelitus. On the diameter of the semicircle, vertically placed with respect to its diameter and equidistantly spaced with respect to its center, two sights were constructed similar to those on the geometrical square. When the semicircle was placed in position on the horizontal limb, the semicircle would project downward and allow this part of the instrument to be turned either in the horizontal or vertical planes. By turning the instrument in the horizontal plane, angles could be read on the theodelitus in degrees or as parts on the geometrical square. On the other hand, when the semicircle was turned in the vertical plane, the angles of

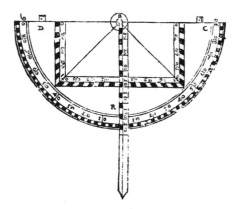

Fig. 16. The vertical circle. From Digges' *Pantometria*.
(Courtesy of the Library of Congress.)

elevation or depression could be read in degrees on the semi-circle or as parts on the geometrical squares constructed within the half circles. In each of these cases the vertical support, mentioned above, acted as an index.

This description of the construction of the topographical instrument shows that it consisted of three essential parts: the geometrical square used as the horizontal limb, the circle of the theodelitus constructed on this limb, and the semicircle attached to the horizontal limb at the center of the theodelitus. This arrangement embodied in principle all the known surveying instruments at that date and constituted a composite instrument by means of which both angles in the horizontal plane and angles of elevation could be determined —the former by the index which moved over the circle of the theodelitus and the latter by the use of the semicircle and double square. Following the descriptions of the construction of the instrument, Digges discusses the appurtenances necessary for its operation.

Digges states[22] that the instrument should be placed on a staff, spiked at one end and equipped with a flat surface at the top on which to set the instrument. This statement indicates that the three-legged tripod had not come into use, nor was there any satisfactory means of joining the instrument to the supporting staff. He also mentions the use of some sort of "needle or flie" to set the diameter of the theodelitus on the North-South meridian; Digges does not state or show in a diagram that this compass was a part of the instrument or that it was attached to the instrument. It is probable that this compass was nothing more than a pocket compass of a type used throughout the sixteenth century.

Examination of a number of Continental instruments constructed during the sixteenth century shows that the fundamental principle and form of the altazimuth theodolite had been developed before the instrument of Digges. The polimetrum of Waldseemüller (see Chapter One) was described and illustrated with a woodcut in the 1512 Strassburg edition of Gregor Reisch's *Margarita Philosophica*. Although Waldseemüller does not give any details of the uses of the polimetrum, this cut shows that it could readily be used for determining horizontal and vertical angles and that it contained many of the fundamental principles which were used by Digges in the "topographicall instrument." Moreover, in the third part of a 1542 manuscript by Jean Roze (Rotz)[23] there is a discussion of the construction and use of an elaborate instrument, the differential quadrant, which embodied the same fundamental principles as Digges' instrument. The differential quadrant was constructed primarily for the accurate determination of the variation of the compass needle,

[22] Digges, *op. cit.*, Chap. 29, Folios F_3^v to F_4^r.
[23] Jean Rotz (fl. 1540–1548) was appointed Hydrographer to the King by Henry VIII in 1542. Taylor, *Mathematical Practitioners*, pp. 169–170.

although it could be readily used to measure horizontal and vertical angles.

While these instruments were being constructed on the Continent, England produced the universal instrument of William Cunningham, described in 1559 in the *Cosmographicall Glasse,* and the instrument of William Bourne, described in a manuscript of about 1570, both of which precede the description of Digges' instruments. It is difficult to determine the exact influence, if any, that these instruments had on Digges, but it seems most probable that Digges would certainly have come into contact—possibly through Dee— with either one or both of these men, their writings, or their instruments. In a discussion of mine-surveying instruments Dunbar Scott has stated:

The English, with pardonable pride, point to the Digges theodelitus as the origin of the theodolite of today; but it does not seem unjust to say that from Digges we have the origin of the theodolite in name only, unless we consider the English cradle-theodolite which certainly had its beginning in the Digges Topographicall Instrument.[24]

Regardless of these facts, it is true that Digges was the first Englishman to explain in print the construction of a simple universal instrument that could be used with a single setting to measure angles in both the horizontal and vertical planes and that it was from this instrument that surveying instruments throughout the world have since been developed. R. T. Gunther believes[25] that Digges had developed his "topographicall instrument" by 1550, but this seems highly improbable since the *Tectonicon* was not published until 1556, and if Digges had had such an instrument fully devel-

[24] Dunbar Scott, "Mine Surveying Instruments," *Transactions Institution Mining Engineers, 23* (1881–1882), 584–591.
[25] R. T. Gunther, "Digges' Theodelitus, The First Booke of the Pantometria," *Old Ashmolean Reprints IV* (Oxford, 1927), Preface.

oped, he would have given some information of the fact in the *Tectonicon*. It seems certain that Digges' "topographicall instrument" was developed some time between 1556, the date of the publication of the *Tectonicon*, and his death in 1560.[26]

For many years it was doubted that any such device as the "topographicall instrument" was ever constructed. However, it has now been definitely established that something of the nature of the topographical instrument was made by Humphrey Cole, probably at Digges' request. Recently, two instruments of this nature have been located. The first, found in the library of St. John's College, Oxford, in a box of rubbish, was examined by Gunther, who believes it to be the oldest theodolite described. This instrument was made by Humphrey Cole[27] and bears the inscription "H+Cole+ 1586." The instrument was incomplete, with the basal alidade and horizontal circle missing, but the vertical semicircle, bearing the maker's name and date, the sighters, and plummet are all extant. The diopter index is 9 inches in length and $\frac{7}{16}$ inches thick and has sights at both ends. These sight vanes are of universal design with right and left brackets at the top; the near vane is perforated with a pinhole, while the foresight has a central bead exactly like that of the foresight of a modern rifle-type sight. The sighter is fixed to the diameter of the vertical semicircle, which is $4\frac{7}{8}$ inches in diameter, its rim being divided into degrees. Inside this semicircle are the scales of *umbra recta* and *umbra versa* which are $2\frac{7}{8}$ inches across and graduated 3–6–9–12–9–6–3. This

---

[26] Louise Diehl Patterson, "Leonard and Thomas Digges, Biographical Notes," *Isis*, *42* (1952), 120–121; and Francis Johnson, "Letters to the Editor," *The Times Literary Supplement* (London, 5 April 1934).

[27] R. T. Gunther, "The Great Astrolabe and Other Scientific Instruments of Humphrey Cole," *Archaeologia*, *29*, 2nd ser. (1929) pp. 273–275.

semicircle turns on an axis and can be clamped in any desired position. The supporting legs are mounted on an arch which carries a small metal plummet over a compass box fitted with two legs and thumbscrews for fitting to a horizontal alidade (now missing) which traverses the horizontal circle. The horizontal alidade and circle have been restored. Gunther states that this is definitely an improved form of the "topographicall instrument" of Digges as previously described and makes the following comment:

The finding of an instrument by Humphrey Cole which combines the Topographicall Instrument of Digges with the added improvement of the Theodolite of Bleau is an historical event of first class importance in the development of instrument construction in the sixteenth century.[28]

The second instrument, now exhibited in the National Maritime Museum, Greenwich, England, although found after the one described above, is of an earlier date. On the horizontal limb the date and signature are H+Cole+1574. A. W. H. Pearsall of the National Maritime Museum states that the instrument (Fig. 17) was complete except for the vertical circle, and this has been restored.[29] This instrument differs but little from the one described by Gunther.

Humphrey Cole, Instrument Maker

It is impossible to discuss the instruments of Leonard Digges and their construction without mention of Humphrey Cole, the distinguished English instrument maker of the sixteenth century. Little is known about Cole's early

[28] R. T. Gunther, *op. cit.;* R. T. Gunther, "The Astrolabe: Its Uses and Derivatives," *The Scottish Geographical Magazine,* 27 (1927), 135–147; and Taylor, *Mathematical Practitioners,* pp. 171–172.
[29] From a letter of A. W. H. Pearsall, Curator of the National Maritime Museum, Greenwich, England, dated 8 December 1959.

Fig. 17. A theodolite by Humphrey Cole. Photograph of the original in the National Maritime Museum at Greenwich, England.
(Courtesy of the Director. Crown copyright reserved.)

life, but he was probably a native of the North of England. He learned engraving on metal and was the first in England to use line engraving on copper plates and to apply this work to geographical purposes. He engraved a map of the Holy Lands for the *Bishops' Bible*, published in 1572 by Richard Jugge; this is probably the first English engraved map to be used in an English book.[30]

Humphrey Cole seems to have been friendly with Leonard Digges and his publisher, Thomas Gemini, who came to England in 1555 or 1556 and was established in Blackfriars, London. Thomas Gemini, Thomas Reynolds, and Humphrey Cole were all experts in copperplate engraving in England. Although the relationship of these three men and Leonard Digges is obscure, it is important. For example, Thomas Gemini published both the *Prognostications* and the *Tectonicon* of Digges. In the colophon of the latter work occurs the statement: "*Tectonicon* imprinted at London by Thomas Gemini . . . who is there ready to make all instruments appertaining to this book." Here it is impossible to determine the exact relationship of Digges, Gemini, the publisher, and Cole, the instrument maker. We do know that Humphrey Cole is mentioned by many of the surveyors, among them William Bourne and Edward Worsop.[31]

Gunther has described in *Archaeologia* a large number of astrolabes and dials made by Cole. According to Gunther,[32] one of these, the Jugge's Universal Portable Dial, comprised all the elements which Cole was likely to have introduced into the horizontal circle of the theodolite. These instru-

[30] R. T. Gunther, "The Great Astrolabe and Other Scientific Instruments of Humphrey Cole," *Archaeologia*, *29*, 2nd ser. (1929), 273–290; *DNB*.

[31] Gunther, *op. cit.*, p. 284; Taylor, *Mathematical Practitioners*, pp. 171–172 and p. 176.

[32] Gunther, *op. cit.*, p. 305.

ments are important in that they show that Cole made use of special devices and gave attention to the practical side of the construction of his instruments. He also displayed an artistic treatment that was not surpassed by any other instrument maker of this period. There is a wide variety of Cole's instruments surviving which includes astrolabes, an armillary sphere, a ring dial, a sector, a nocturnal, a geometrical table, and parts of two theodolites. These instruments reveal the ingenuity of Cole as an instrument maker and the position that English instrument designing had reached by the end of the sixteenth century through the efforts of Leonard Digges and Humphrey Cole.[33]

Valentine Leigh

The instruments described and constructed by Digges did not immediately come into use by the practical land surveyors. Following the works of Digges—that is, during the second half of the sixteenth century—four texts on surveying were published. One was on instruments, and another was devoted to surveyor's errors. The former was published in London in 1577 by Valentine Leigh[34] with the title, *The Most Profitable and Commendable Science of Surveying of Landes, Tenemens, and Hereditamentes.* The book consists of a title page, fifty-nine folios, and two large tables; it is printed in black letter and illustrated with thirty-one well-

[33] J. O. Halliwell, *A Collection of Letters Concerning the Progress of Science in England* (London, 1841), p. 18; Gunther, *op. cit.,* pp. 273–317; Taylor, *Mathematical Practitioners,* pp. 171–172.
[34] Valentine Leigh flourished from 1560 to 1590; by profession a surveyor, he wrote on miscellaneous topics. He belongs to the old school of surveyors who distinguish between the surveyor who drew up the terrier of the manor and the landmeater who usually handled the measuring rods or lines. *DNB;* and Taylor, *Mathematical Practitioners,* p. 174.

drawn figures. In the sixteenth century there were at least four editions or reprints.

Leigh attempts in this book to combine into one single text the two elements required of the early surveyor and expressed more or less separately in the works of Master Fitzherbert and Richard Benese. At the outset he defines the duties of the sixteenth-century surveyor, pointing out that it was not enough for the land surveyor to be able to measure land, but that he should also be able to give the lord of the manor all information pertaining to the manor. He sets out the surveyor's duties as follows:

1. He should know what is meant by a manor; that is, what constitutes a manor.
2. He should know and consider all rents and holdings on the manor.
3. He should be able to perform the practical survey or measurements of the manor; that is, to give the buttes and bounds and to make a plot of the whole manor.
4. He should have a fair knowledge of the common law as applied to estates and manors.

In line with the above qualifications, it was necessary for the surveyor to give a complete accounting of the estate to the lord or his agents. This accounting, to be prepared and put into book form, was usually called the customary roll. Leigh refers the reader to the works of Master Fitzherbert for a more detailed account of the customary rolls for details relating to this part of the survey. He adds, however, that the customary rolls should give the following information:

1. the true value of all lands;
2. the amount of all rents, fines, and fees arising from the estate or manor; and
3. any and all deductions with respect to the manor.

After the discussion of the customary roll, Leigh gives detailed instructions for the survey. The surveyor should first "vewe and survey the Buttes and Bounds of the whole Manour" and then measure the buttes and bounds of every parcel of the land. Referring to the measuring instruments, he states:

> To aunswere by Rodde or by line, it is at your pleasure but of them both the lyne is the spedier and most commodious, and also of most antiquitie.

> Your line beyng foure Perches of lengthe, and at euery perche end a knot, would be well seared with hoate Waxe and Rosen, auoide stretching thereof in the wete, and shrinking in the drought.[35]

The author also suggests that the surveyor carry "a Diall in your hande (according to Maister Fitzherbertes counsaile)" so that he may know perfectly which is east, west, south, or north.[36]

For each and every field the surveyor should stand in the center of the field and look over the whole ground to be surveyed. Survey measurements should be written in a "paperbooke" so that the data would not be lost, as they would be if recorded on a single sheet of paper. The surveyor should also include all information relative to each parcel of land, giving not only the buttes and bounds but also the area of the parcels, the number of houses on each parcel and where they are located, the amount of timber, the minerals, the number of mills, and any other pertinent

[35] Leigh, *The Most Profitable and Commendable Science of Surveying, of Landes, Tenemens, and Hereditamentes*, Folio O.ᵛ. It is possible that this is the source of Edmund Gunter's chain of four rods or perches.

[36] Diall here, no doubt, refers to a hand or pocket magnetic compass.

facts. This additional information may be included with the customary rolls or set down in a separate roll or form.

For the computation of areas Leigh goes into somewhat more detail than either Fitzherbert or Benese, first giving the areas of simple right-lined figures. Although anyone might follow the works of Architas, Archimedes, and Euclid on geometry, he refers the reader to the works of Richard Benese and Leonard Digges for the actual computation of the areas of the parcels of land.[37] However, since these books may not be accessible, he gives a resumé of their principles and also some examples illustrating the methods used in those works.

Following the discussion of the computation of the area of land in terms of acres and parts of acres, Leigh suggests that one should always consider the type of land that is being cast up, because woodlands are measured with a rod or perch of a different length from the perch used for arable land. He then discusses finding the areas of various types of figures, including rectangles, polygons, and the like. In particular he states:

> Yet alwaies must such peeces of Lande whatsoever it bee, bee reduced into one certaine breadth and one certaine length, or else it can neuer bee collected or summed into a perfecte contente or number of Acres, and other odde quantities.[38]

If the figures contain sides or boundaries that are not straight lines, these should be enclosed in a rectangle; next, the excluded area of the field should be combined with the additional area included by the rectangle—but the author does not tell us how this is to be done. Leigh then considers the areas of hills and valleys, and in doing so follows Benese

[37] Leigh, *op. cit.*, Folios O_2^r to O_3^v.
[38] Leigh, *op. cit.*, Folio O_3^r.

in finding the lateral or superficial area instead of the plan area. At the close of the discussion of areas are two tables for finding the acres and parts of acres when the length and breadth of the given piece of ground are known. On the other hand, the author is none too clear in his discussion of the measuring of the manor, for he gives the barest details in this important part of the work. Leigh does suggest that a map should be given with the completed work of the survey, but again there are no instructions for its construction.

This text of Leigh is the last attempt of a sixteenth-century surveyor to combine into one text the duties of the land steward along with the work of the land surveyor.

Edward Worsop

In 1582 there appeared a book by Edward Worsop which is one of the most interesting texts of the sixteenth century, comprising as it does a discussion of the errors and short-comings of the contemporary surveyor.[39] The complete title gives an idea of the scope of the book:

A Discoverie of sundrie errours and faults daily committed by Landemeaters, ignorant of Arithmeticke and Geometrie, to the damage, and preiudice of many of her Maiesties subiects, with Manifest proofe that none ought to be admitted to that function, but the learned practitioners of those Sciences.

This book of eighty folios is printed in black letter, and there is no evidence that it passed through more than one edition.

In the dedication the author gives his reasons and qualifications for writing the book. He states that the works of Euclid, Robert Recorde, Leonard and Thomas Digges, and

[39] Edward Worsop, *A Discoverie of Sundrie Errours and Faults Daily Committed by Landemeaters* (London, 1582).

others are available but are written in such technical language that the average surveyor or land measurer is unable to understand them. It is his intention to write a text without technical details—one that will point out the errors made by many surveyors—and then to indicate the proper procedure in measuring the boundaries of parcels of land and in computing the areas of these parcels. Instead of giving geometrical theorems with rigorous proofs, Worsop states the general principles of arithmetic and geometry and then explains how these may be correctly used by surveyors.[40] In the introduction he also gives the names of some of the most important instrument makers of that time, among them the well-known names of Humphrey Cole, John Read, and John Reynolds.[41]

The importance of this work lies largely in its being the first of a series of surveying texts to follow Robert Recorde's method of writing in dialogue form. It is also the earliest work on surveying that is primarily concerned with the detailed errors committed by surveyors and land measurers. The discussion takes place between M. Peter; Iohnson, a clothier; Worsop, a surveyor; M. Watkins; and Stevens, a serving man. With different members of this group Worsop discusses the various aspects of a survey, pointing out the varying lengths of the perch and rod used in England at this time.[42] He is emphatic in his statements that the areas of

[40] Worsop, *op. cit.*, Folios A_2^r to A_4^v.

[41] John Read (fl. 1582–1610), instrument maker, frequently mentioned by Worsop, Lucar, and Blagrave should not be confused with his nephew of the same name, an instrument maker about 1660. John Read, senior, was one of the notable instrument makers of the late sixteenth century and specialized in making plane tables. John Read, junior, was the partner and then the successor of the noted instrument maker, John Thompson. Taylor, *Mathematical Practitioners*, pp. 185 and 237.

[42] Worsop states that the 18-foot perch was generally used for woodland measure throughout England, but that the 11-foot perch was

two parcels of land are in the same ratio as the lengths of the rods used in measuring the sides. In this connection he goes into much detail concerning the cords, wires, and rods used by surveyors, explaining their construction and discussing the inaccuracies caused by faulty construction.

Worsop's chief criticism of the sixteenth-century surveyor is his ignorance of the fundamental principles of arithmetic and geometry. At the beginning of the discussion he states that he will not attempt to give proofs of the geometrical theorems, but demonstrations and illustrations of the errors as well as the correct procedures for working the various problems. He then points out four frequent errors committed by land measurers. First is the practice of many surveyors of laying head to head; that is, of multiplying the length by the width of a four-sided figure without considering whether or not the angles are right angles. The second error has to do with measuring by the eye; that is, the surveyor determines the size of the angle by inspection and without any instrument. The third error is made in determining the areas of irregular figures. Many surveyors combine the lengths of all the sides, divide by four, and then square this result to obtain the true area. In the case of an irregular field, the surveyors frequently measure a square inside the boundary of the field, compute the area of the square, and then "estimate by the eye" the amount that should be added to the area of the square to give the area of the parcel of land. The fourth error is taking the circumference of a circular piece of ground, dividing it by four, and then squaring this result to obtain the area.

In order to correct the faults and deficiencies of the surveyors, Worsop suggests that experts in the several fields

---

not used near London. He gave the opinion that this measure was used "far from London in some Manors, that measure is allowed of, and is called in some places, tenant right, in other some, curt measure." Worsop, *op. cit.*, Folio B$_2^v$.

of surveying should take the time to train and examine every surveyor. Then it would be possible to license the surveyors in the same manner as in other professions. He proposes that the English government should encourage and promote the study of mathematics by subsidizing and supporting eminent mathematicians, as was being done on the Continent.

In closing the discussion Worsop states that surveying consists of three parts: mathematical, legal, and judicial. The mathematical part consists of the measuring of the sides and location of the boundaries, the calculation of the areas, and the construction of the plot. The legal side pertains to the keeping of the rolls of the court of survey, tenures, services, and all information regarding the tenants and persons connected with the manor. For these matters, Worsop refers the reader to the works of Master Fitzherbert and Valentine Leigh. The third and final part of surveying, the judicial, is the consideration of the facts relating to the fertility of the soil, the value of the buildings, and a careful consideration of the facts relating to both the lord and the tenants, since the surveyor should be a friend of the tenant as well as of the lord.[43]

Worsop's work is principally concerned with the errors committed by the practicing surveyors. This is the principal contribution of Worsop. In contrast the next publication deals with methods of surveying and a description of instruments generally used by surveyors in the last half of the sixteenth century.

Cyprian Lucar

The second highly practical surveying text written in the sixteenth century was by Cyprian Lucar and was published in London in 1690.[44] It bore the title, *A Treatise Named*

---

[43] Worsop, *op. cit.*, Folio E₃ʳ.

[44] Cyprian Lucar (b. 1544, fe. 1590) is usually classed as a mathematician and author. In 1588 he published *Three Bookes of Colloquies*

Lucar Solace. On the title page Lucar states that the text was "in part collected out of diuerse languages, and in part by Cyprian Lucar, Gentleman." The text discusses four main heads: definitions and measures; the general principles of the survey; the construction of geometrical figures, plotting, and the computation of areas; and finally a section devoted to the valuation of land, building of houses and roads, leveling, drainage, and the supplying of water to houses.

Lucar's survey is essentially the plane-table type — he uses the plane table to determine not only horizontal distances but also altitudes and depressions. In these cases the board is turned sidewise and the plotting done in this position. In order to determine the altitude of hills or to obtain the distance of inaccessible objects, Lucar uses two stations and the measured distance between the two stations. With these measurements at his disposal it was possible for the surveyor to determine any other distance and in particular the altitude and slope lines. The slope line was important in sixteenth- and seventeenth-century surveying, inasmuch as the superficial area of a hill or valley was used instead of the plane area.

To determine the horizontal distance between two inaccessible points, Lucar uses either one station and two measured distances or two stations and one measured distance. For the first case he protracts on paper a triangle of the distances; in the second case a quadrilateral of the distances is protracted. In both cases, however, the required distance can be determined with a small amount of arithmetical calculation. When surveying a field, manor, or large tract of

---

Concerning the Art of Shooting in Great and Small Pieces of Artillerie. This work was a translation of the work of the Italian, Nicholas Tartaglia (*ca.* 1500–1557). *DNB;* Joseph Foster, *Alumni Oxonienses* (London, 1891) 1500–1714; Taylor, *Tudor Geography,* pp. 46–47; Taylor, *Mathematical Practitioners,* pp. 176–177.

land, Lucar first goes around all the sides and sets up stakes with white paper or cloth at each of the corners. He then sets his plane table at each station or corner and sights the next station, plotting the angle and distances on the paper fastened to the board, the distances having been previously measured with a wire line, cord, or chain. If one or more of the sides are curved, he sets up stakes rather close together, depending on how much the side is curved, and then measures straight lines between these stakes. When other cases arise, he uses two stations and sights all the corners; by measuring one distance he is able to protract and determine the lengths of all the distances. This method of surveying is a form of triangulation survey, but it was not explained or used to any great extent until the seventeenth century.

In determining the area of land Lucar first gives rules for computing the areas of different types of figures—triangles, quadrilaterals of all types, and circles. For these computations he uses the measured and protracted distances of the various figures. Lucar states that he is using the rules for determining the areas that had previously been given by Benese, Digges, and Leigh. He makes a careful distinction in the calculated areas between those acres measured in statute perches and those measured in customary perches.

The protraction of areas and figures is dealt with more thoroughly by Lucar than by any previous writer of the sixteenth century. He first considers the geometrical figures such as triangles and circles and the dividing of a line into a given number of parts, which is used in a method for dividing a given piece of land into two or more parts where each has a given area. The protraction of surveyed land is usually done by Lucar on the plane table while the survey is taking place. In this method one or two distances are measured, the direction of other points are determined on the paper of the plane table, and then with the compasses and the scale

79

the lines are all drawn and the distances are determined with a small amount of arithmetical calculation.

Lucar's work is important for several reasons. One contribution is the description of the instruments that the average land surveyor should have in his possession (Fig. 18). He gives a careful description of the 4-perch line and the geometrical or plane table and an explanation of its uses. For the line, a good piece of wire should be purchased and then divided by means of a carpenter's rule into 4-perch lengths, then into ½- and ¼-perches, and further into 1-foot lengths. All of these divisions are then distinguished from one another by being painted different colors.

Lucar gives the first description in English of the plane table, which he describes as being rectangular in shape, with

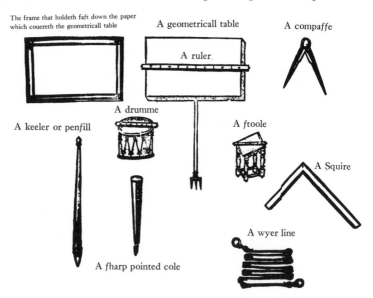

Fig. 18. Surveying instruments described by Lucar. From Lucar's *Lucar Solace*.
(Courtesy of the Henry Huntington Library.)

a frame to hold the paper and with some form of ruler or index. If a plane table is not available, he says that a stool, drum, or any other object with a flat surface might be used. Although he warns that the instrument should be level with the horizontal, he does not give any instructions for leveling. It should be possible, he adds, to turn the plane table over, so that it can be used in the vertical plane. This is the first mention in an English surveying text of the ball-and-socket arrangement for turning an instrument on a staff or support. Lucar also improves the staff or tripod to support instruments. The support previously used had been constructed of a single rod of wood or iron, pointed at one end so that it could be forced into the ground. Lucar, however, attached near the end of this rod a rectangular piece of wood perpendicular to the rod, and to this were affixed three short, pointed pieces which could be forced into the ground. This arrangement not only gave greater support to the instrument, but also allowed the operator to level it to the horizontal plane with greater ease.

Lucar also used a sight rule that was unique with the sixteenth-century surveyor, one that may have suggested the form of the telescope used on instruments when the telescope reached the proper stage of development. This sight rule or index was made of two thin strips of wood, with a small groove cut longitudinally and parallel to the edges of each strip. The two strips were then glued together, giving a small tube through which one might sight distant objects.

Ralph Agas

The final[45] work on surveying in the sixteenth century was unusual in that it was the published notes of a surveyor. Since the publication was small, a 20-page pamphlet, it could be

[45] A text on surveying reportedly published in 1589 by John Farmery, "practitioner in Physic," does not seem to be extant.

carried in the pocket and used as a handbook during the course of the survey. The text was prepared by Ralph Agas[46] and published in London in 1596 with the title, *A Preparative to Plotting of Lands and Tenementes for Surveighs*. Apparently the author had the book printed primarily for his own use, for Agas states that it would have required too much time to prepare a full-length text on the subject. The tract is printed in black letter, paged but not foliated; it apparently passed through only one edition.

In this short treatise the author does not discuss elaborate details of the survey, of finding areas, or of plotting; on the other hand, he goes into detail with regard to the best types of instrument to use, their uses, and the shortcomings of contemporary surveys.

Agas' is the first surveying text to state that the author had used one of the surveying instruments devised by Leonard Digges. Agas says that he had been a surveyor for thirty years and that for twenty-five years of that time he had used the plane table, with and without the needle, but that he had found within the last five years that the plane table was highly unsatisfactory for large tracts of land. He states that he had found the theodolite preferable to any other instrument for surveying of this type. The instrument that Agas refers to as the theodolite or "sphericall instrument" is without doubt a modified form of the "topographicall instrument" of Leonard Digges. This is probably the first time that the term theodolite was applied to the "topographicall

---

[46] Ralph or Radulph Agas (1545–1621) is usually classed as a land surveyor and engraver. Agas began surveying at an early age, probably about 1566, and during his lifetime he surveyed and drew plans of Cambridge, Oxford, and London. Agas was one of the earliest English surveyors to use the plane table and to adopt the theodolite after a description had been given by Thomas Digges. *DNB;* Hugh James Rose, *New Biographical Dictionary* (London, 1850); and Taylor, *Mathematical Practitioners*, p. 177.

instrument." Along with the theodolite, Agas mentions that he has used the circumferentor in his surveys, also the first specific reference to that instrument in a surveying text. In several documents which he wrote and left in manuscript form, Agas gives a more complete description of some of the instruments and methods that he used in the survey. In one of these he mentions a theodolite 20 inches in diameter and adds, "the measure attendinge uppon this instrument is of steele wier toe pole longe lincked foote by foote, except for the halfe foote at either ende."[47] In the discussion of the survey, Agas is the first author to state the use of one station inside a large piece of land in conducting the survey.

The improved methods of surveying proposed by Worsop, Lucar, and Agas began to suggest the need for scales that would read rectilinear distances and angular measurements with greater ease and accuracy. In order to meet this need, the instrument makers began to adopt the suggestions of the earlier writers and to borrow methods from the astronomers for the construction of scales for reading distances and angles easily and accurately.

Circular Divisions

Division of the arc of a circle into a given number of equal parts has never been an easy task, and we are not very familiar with early methods of doing it. One of the earliest methods for dividing the degrees of the circular arc into smaller parts was that of Pedro Núñez (1502–1578), described in his *De crepusculis Liber Unus*, published at Lisbon in 1542. By this method 44 concentric arcs were drawn within the graduated arc of a quadrant, the outer arc being divided into degrees. These inner arcs, beginning with the

[47] *DNB.*, under Agas; and Taylor, *Mathematical Practitioners*, pp. 177 and 333.

one next to the graduated arc were then divided into 89, 88, 87, . . . , and 46 equal divisions respectively. With such a large number of divisions the alidade of the instrument was almost sure to touch a division mark on one of the 45 concentric circles. The angle was then determined by the solution of a simple proportion. This device was usually known as the *nonius*.

Although the nonius is relatively simple, the problem of dividing the large number of circles into their various parts offered difficulties which were not easily overcome at this period of instrument development. As a consequence the nonius was little used, but by a strange misunderstanding the term has been and still is frequently applied to the vernier, with which it has nothing in common.[48] In Dudley's *Arcano del Mare*, published in Florence in 1646, there is an example (Fig. 19) of a quadrant divided by the method of Nũnez.

At the time the nonius was being developed, another method of dividing circular arcs and linear scales was devised and used with considerable success during the latter part of the sixteenth and early seventeenth centuries. This was the method of transversals or diagonal scales, and its first use in the straight line division on the cross-staff is generally credited to Levi ben Gerson.[49] It is possible in Central Europe that both Purbach and Regiomontanus knew the method of transversals, for Kästner states that Puchner described the method in his work on geometry in 1561, and

[48] R. T. Gunther, *Early Science at Oxford* (Oxford, 1922), Part II, p. 81.

[49] Levi ben Gerson (1288–1344) was one of the leading Jewish mathematicians of the fourteenth century. He is credited with the invention of the Jacob's or cross-staff. A. von Braunmuhl, *Vorlesungen über die Geschichte der Trigonometrie* (Leipzig, 1900) Part I, pp. 103–107, and Siegmund Gunter, Die Erfindung des Baculum Geometricus *Bibliotheca Mathematica* (1885), Vol. 2, pp. 137 ff.

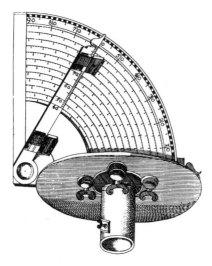

Fig. 19. Dudley's quadrant with nonius. From Dudley's *Arcano del Mare*.
(Courtesy of the New York Public Library.)

Tycho Brahe obtained a cross-staff divided by this method in 1562.[50]

On the other hand, in 1573 Thomas Digges gave a drawing of a rectilinear scale divided by means of transversals with which he divided a cross-staff. He states this method was first applied to the cross-staff by Richard Chanzler, an English instrument maker.[51] These transversals consisted of three different arrangements: one with diagonal lines sloping in both directions, another with a diagonal line of dots

[50] A. G. Kästner, *Geschichte der Mathematik* (Göttingen, 1796–1800) Vol. 3, p. 479; Christopher Clovius, *Operum Mathematicorum* (Magvntiae, 1611), Vol. 3, pp. 10–12, 33–39; and Johannes A. Repsold, *Zur Geschichte der Astronomischen Messwerkzeuge von Puerbach bis Reichenbach, 1450–1830* (Leipzig, 1908).

[51] Thomas Digges, *Alae seu Scalae Mathematicae* (London, 1573), Folio I.

sloping in both directions, and the third a diagonal line of dots sloping in one direction only (Fig. 20). Gunther believes that the elaborate tables developed by Purbach and Regiomontanus suggested and necessitated an attempt to increase the instrumental accuracy of the late sixteenth century, particularly in astronomical instruments and, carried over into the seventeenth century, in surveying instruments.[52]

The Close of the Century

The sixteenth century had opened with the publication of the first two printed English texts on surveying. One, by Fitzherbert, gave the duties of the land steward, stated how the manor should be managed, and included some slight discussion of the actual measuring of land. The other, by Benese, was devoted almost entirely to the measuring of land. These two texts passed through a number of printings in the sixteenth century and exerted considerable influence on several texts that followed in the latter half of the same century.

Texts of the second half of the sixteenth century began to show the scientific growth of the art of the surveyor. The works of Leonard and Thomas Digges gave a description and explanation of the uses of the instruments then available for the use of the surveyor as well as a new instrument, the "topographicall instrument," a composite of several other existing instruments. There followed several texts which gave in more detailed fashion the work of the surveyor in measuring, casting up his area, and plotting his results on paper. Some of these, that by Worsop in particular, began to point out the shortcomings of the surveyor, directing at-

[52] Gunther, *Early Science at Oxford*, Part II, pp. 82–84.

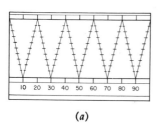

(a)

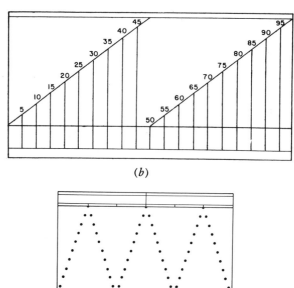

(b)

(c)

Fig. 20. Diagrams illustrating the method of division of linear
and circular scales;
(a) Thomas Digges,
(b) Richard Chanzler, and
(c) Tycho Brahe.
Redrawn from Thomas Digges' *Alae seu Scalae Mathematicae*.
      (Courtesy of the Library of Congress.)

87

tention to the particular errors that were being made and in some cases making definite suggestions for improvements.

In instrument construction and operation greater use was made during the second half of the century of the instruments developed in central Europe and in England during the fifteenth and early part of the sixteenth centuries. Among these was an adaptation of the astrolabe, the geometrical square, and the cross-staff for surveying purposes. Invention of the plane table brought into being a new instrument with its possibilities for surveying and plotting in the field. Construction of the theodelitus and "topographicall instrument" by Digges marked the beginning of the development of modern instrument design not only in England but throughout the civilized world. Although the full impact of the development of these instruments was not felt until the latter part of the seventeenth and early eighteenth centuries, they did produce a change in the whole of instrument construction before that time. Several other instruments were developed during the century, in particular the staff of Blagrave, but on the whole these were short-lived and served only a particular need at the time of their invention.

Although used little on surveying instruments in England during the sixteenth century, the nonius and the method of transversals were known by the close of the century, at any rate to some of the English instrument makers. During the last decade of the century the defects of the plane table had been recognized by some of the surveyors, and the possibilities of the theodolite for use in large and small surveys had been demonstrated. In other words, by the close of the sixteenth century the search for a universal instrument for angle measurements had almost been completed. For distance measurements little or nothing had been accomplished, except for occasional unimportant changes in the length of the same rod or line which had been used since the Middle Ages.

In the survey itself considerable progress was made. With the increase in the value of land and with a greater demand for agricultural products there was an ever-increasing need by both the lord of the manor and the tenant for more accurate surveys. These improved surveys were made possible by the adaptation of the new instruments of the sixteenth century and of the more refined methods of surveying. The most obvious of these new methods was that of triangulation with one or two fixed stations. An effort was made on the part of the surveyors to prepare accurate and factual maps or plats of the survey.

By the close of the sixteenth century English surveying had developed far beyond that of the ancients. In instrument construction the designers and makers were able to design and construct workable instruments embodying the fundamental principles of Hero's dioptra. English instrument makers had also utilized the discoveries and techniques of the sixteenth-century instrument craftsmen of Continental Europe.

In surveying methods the surveyors had improved the old methods and had utilized the new method of triangulation of large tracts of land. Furthermore, surveyors were supplied with a small but adequate supply of texts on the subject. The profession was now ready for further advances in surveying itself and in the training of its practitioners.

The Seventeenth Century

Educational Background

Although mathematical education had made some progress in England from 1500 to 1600, instruction in these subjects was still very poor at the beginning of the seventeenth century. The influences of Robert Recorde in arithmetic and of John Dee and Leonard and Thomas Digges in practical mathematics played an important part in the development of science in general and surveying in particular. As time went on, several advances in practical mathematics were made in the seventeenth century: the study of trigonometry was introduced in the universities,[1] logarithms were discovered during the early part of the century, and the study of geometry was emphasized. However, many seventeenth-century scientists were self-educated in applied mathematics, for instruction in mathematics and applied sciences in the universities was still almost nil.

Information relating to mathematical instruction is frequently obtained from advertisements of private teachers or

[1] L. C. Karpinski, "Biographical Check List of all Works on Trigonometry Published up to 1700 A.D.," *Scripta Mathematica, 12,* (1924), 267–283.

from the instructions to the professors of mathematics in the universities. Henry Saville, in his regulations drawn up for Oxford University in 1619, states: "It will, besides, be the duty of the Geometry professor to teach and expound Arithmetic of all kinds, both speculative and practical; land-surveying and practical geometry . . . ," and again, "He shall show the practice of geometry to his auditors (who choose to attend him) in the field or spots adjacent to the University."[2] Conditions at Cambridge were little different from those at Oxford. The biographer of Seth Ward, an English clergyman and astronomer who entered Sidney Sussex College, Cambridge, in 1632, reports that by chance Seth Ward found some books on mathematics in the library but that he was unable to find any one of the fellows in the college to instruct him in those subjects.[3]

In surveying, instruction was either private or by apprenticeship. The personal advertisements of many of the private teachers give some information of the instruction in surveying. One such notice by Thomas Bretnor in his *A Newe Almanacke for 1616* states that "These Arts following are taught in English, Latine, French, and Spanish . . . Geometry . . . surveying of lands &c with many instruments. . . ."[4] Several other teachers who taught land measuring are mentioned in surveying texts, among them Henry Lyte (fl. 1620) and John Spiedell (fl. 1630).

In many cases the surveyors were self-taught both in mathematics and surveying. A striking example is Richard Norwood (1590–1675), who had little formal education

[2] G. R. M. Ward, *Oxford University Statutes* (London, 1875), Vol. 1, pp. 273–274.
[3] Walter Pope, *Life of Right Reverend Seth, Lord Bishop of Salisbury* (London, 1697), p. 9.
[4] Thomas Bretnor, *A Newe Almanacke for 1616* (London, 1616), p. 6. Bretnor, who flourished between 1607 and 1618, was a mathematician, almanac maker, and teacher in London. *DNB*.

but gained his mathematical and surveying training from private study while a young man at sea. He states that he made constant use of Recorde's *Arithmetic* and Leonard Digges's *Tectonicon* and *Pantometria*.[5] Another such self-taught man was Adam Martindale, a late seventeenth-century teacher and surveyor. His biography states that at the age of forty he "knew little of more than arithmetic in a vulgar way and decimals in Jager's bungling method," so that he then began the study of decimals, algebra, and logarithms in an earnest manner.[6]

During the last half of the seventeenth century five important new texts on surveying were published in addition to reprints and revisions of some of the sixteenth-century texts. Although three of these five texts were written within two years of each other, they were quite different and discuss different aspects of surveying.

John Norden

The first surveying publication of the seventeenth century is the *Surveiors Dialogue* published in 1607 in London by I(John) Norden[7] and republished in 1610 with the addition of a sixth book or chapter. It is the second surveying text to be written in dialogue form, and consists of a discussion

[5] Richard Norwood, *The Journal of Richard Norwood*, with an introduction by Wesley Frank Craven and Walter B. Haywood (New York, 1946), pp. 40–45.

[6] Richard Parkinson, ed., *The Life of Adam Martindale*, written by himself. Printed for the Chatham Society (London, 1845), p. 200.

[7] John Norden (1548–1625) is usually a topographer. In 1606 he was Crown Surveyor of woods in several counties of England. In 1607 he surveyed Windsor, and thereafter he was frequently employed for the King's surveys. Several contemporaries bear the same name, and much confusion has arisen therefrom. *DNB.*; J. Grainger, *Biographical History of England* 3rd ed. (London, 1799); Taylor, *Mathematical Practitioners*, p. 177.

among the surveyor, a farmer, the lord of the manor, a bailiff, and a purchaser. The first section in the surveyor's discussion with the farmer points out the need for surveys and clears up the dissatisfaction with the surveyor on the part of the farmer and the tenant. The farmer feels that surveying is a recent innovation by the lord of the manor to obtain greater rents from his tenants, a feeling expressed in his statement, "But I Maruaille how such great persons did before Surueying came up: for this is an upstart art found out of late, both measuring and plotting."[8] On the other hand, the surveyor explains to the tenant that the value of grain has increased in equal or greater proportion with respect to rents, and therefore the land is more valuable, requiring more accurate surveys. The author then reminds the lord of his obligations to his tenants.

Norden closes the discussion with the bailiff by stating that unless the surveyor holds his office by patent, by commission out of the Chancery or Exchequer, Duchy Court, or Court of Wards, he cannot administer an oath when he calls the court of survey. If he cannot administer an oath, then the surveyor must have the bailiff call the court and administer all oaths. Norden goes into much detail on the legal technicalities of conducting the court and the survey. After the court of survey has been adjourned, the surveyor may go ahead and make his perambulations, or conduct the survey.

In the discussion of the survey Norden explains, for the first time in an English text, the difference between the theodolite and the circumferentor, stating that the circumferentor is nothing more than a new name given to a form of the theodolite. In the case of the theodolite, the needle always remains over the North-South meridian and the index or sights are turned about, whereas in the circumferentor the index or sights are fixed to the instrument which

[8] John Norden, *Surveiors Dialogue*, Folio D_2^v.

is turned about until the sights are fixed on the line of the course. Then the angle is marked off by the "wandering needle" and is read on the card in the compass box.[9]

Norden's surveyor goes around the entire manor and then around each field using the plane table, although he points out that other instruments may be used. In this discussion he mentions backsighting each station that he has passed. This is the first mention of backsighting in an English text, although Norden does not explain the purpose or use to be made of this reading. In the notebook he shows not only the measurements of the field's dimensions but also the tenant's names and other information regarding the fields and the land. For woodland, the surveyor should count the trees on a small square; after the area of the woodland has been determined he will then be able to calculate the approximate number of trees on a given area.

After giving the necessary geometry relating to various types of figures, the author explains how land area may be found. In general, for irregular tracts of land he divides the figure into a series of triangles and trapezoids and, by protraction, determines the sides of the divisions. He then uses a table to find the areas of the figures and adds these partial areas to find the total. His tables, he explains, were taken from the texts of Benese, Leigh, and Digges.

Norden's work is the last of the surveying texts to be written in dialogue form. This text is important because of Norden's clear account of the operation of the court of survey and because of his efforts to reconcile the differences between surveyor and tenant. His methods are generally superior to those given by sixteenth-century writers on surveying.

---

[9] Norden, *op. cit.*, Folio S_1^v. In this discussion the theodolite mentioned is not to be confused with the topographical instrument.

Arthur Hopton

The second important surveyor of the seventeenth century to publish a text was Arthur Hopton, whose *Speculum Topographicum* (1611)[10] gave a general description of all the surveying instruments in use at that time. Hopton, like many other surveyors and instrument makers, attempted to utilize the advances in instrument construction made by Leonard Digges or to modify the instruments of Digges to suit his own ideas.

Hopton's contribution to the instruments of the early part of the seventeenth century was what he called the *topographical glasses*. Although this instrument was not used to any extent except by Hopton and a few other surveyors, its construction and design show the influence of Leonard Digges and others and also the efforts of its designer to construct a single instrument that would perform several tasks at the same time with a fair degree of accuracy. Compared with modern surveying instruments, the topographical glasses might be regarded as a monstrosity, but the instrument was based on certain fundamental principles which had not been used, or at least had not been explained in English, in connection with a surveying instrument.

The topographical glasses consisted of a planisphere (Fig. 21*a*), a circle with indices and sights (Fig. 21*b*) to fit within the planisphere, a vertical circle (Fig. 21*c*) made so that it could be attached to one set of indices, the compass card (Fig. 21*d*), and a compass box and needle (Fig. 21*e*). The planisphere was divided into various scales,

[10] Arthur Hopton, *Speculum Topographicum: or the Topographicall Glasses* (London, 1611) Hopton (1588-1614) was educated at Lincoln College, Oxford. From Oxford he entered Clement's Inn in London as a surveyor and mathematical practitioner. He took pupils, wrote almanacs, designed instruments, and wrote books on their uses. Hugh James Rose, *New General Biographical Dictionary* (London, 1850); Taylor, *Mathematical Practitioners*, p. 200.

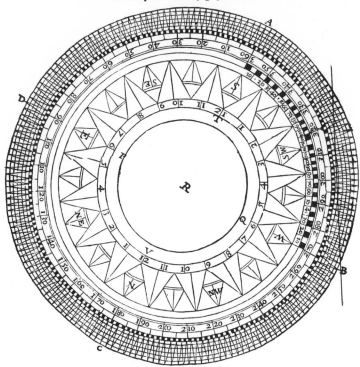

The Planisphere of the Topographicall Glasse.

Place this Shéete betwéene the folioes of 16. and 17.

(a)

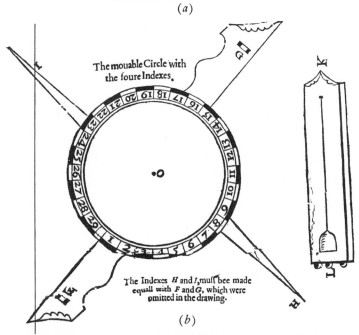

The mouable Circle with
the foure Indexes.

The Indexes H and I, must bee made
equall with F and G, which were
omitted in the drawing.

(b)

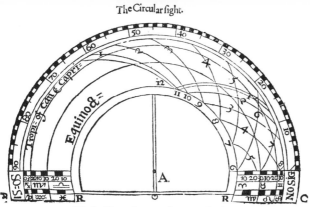

The Circular sight.

The Antickes, or Supporters here are omitted.

(c)

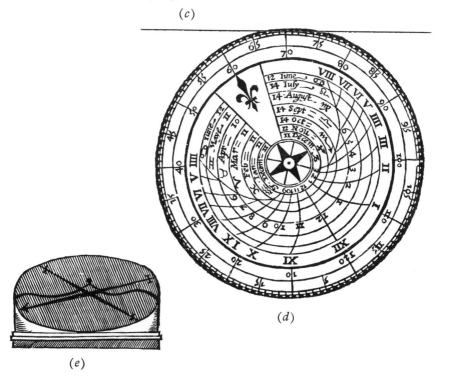

(d)

(e)

Fig. 21. The unassembled parts of the topographical glass of
Hopton;
(a) the planisphere or limb,
(b) the movable circle and sights,
(c) the vertical semicircle,
(d) the compass card, and
(e) the compass box with needle.
From Hopton's *Topographicall Glasses*.
(Courtesy of the Library of Congress.)

reading from the center outwards: a cutout portion, a circular space divided into 24 spaces, a division of the circle into the 32 winds, a division of the quadrant of the circle divided from 0′ to 120° and then to 0° to represent the geometrical square, and finally the circle divided into 360°. About ½-inch from this circle another circle is drawn. Within the two circles are drawn five concentric equispaced circles. An isosceles triangle is constructed on each two degrees making it possible to read the angle to 10′ of the arc. This is the first instance in an English surveying text of the diagonal divisions of the circular scale. When assembled, the result was an instrument not only similar to Digges' topographical instrument but an astronomical instrument as well. In explaining the needle, to be used with the compass box and card, the author states that the needle is made by combining two needles at right angles for the purpose of making the needle steadier. This arrangement would seem to introduce difficulties which are not mentioned or explained. The author does state, however, that if one end of the needle is made heavier than the other, and if the needle is of sufficient length, its dip will be compensated. Because of its length, the needle can be used to level the instrument in the horizontal plane.

Hopton's description of the support for the instrument is the first mention by an English surveyor of the three-legged tripod, first described in 1579 by Philip Danfrie, a French instrument maker. In addition, Hopton gives an excellent description of a ball-and-socket arrangement for attaching the instrument to the tripod, this again being the first instance of a description in an English surveying text of a ball-and-socket arrangement.

Hopton also suggests that his topographical glasses could be easily converted into a plane table by removing the sights, turning the planisphere over, and using the reverse side.

Nevertheless, Hopton gives a description of the plane table that was in use at that time. This table was made of three smooth boards about 12 inches long clamped together by means of a frame divided on each side into 100 equal parts. If a compass box was used, it was fastened on one side of the table so that the North-South line of the compass card was parallel to a side of the table. The ruler and sights (Fig. 22) are typical of those used throughout the seventeenth century on the plane table.

Although mentioned by Ralph Agas in the sixteenth century and by John Norden early in the seventeenth century, the circumferentor used continuously throughout the seventeenth and eighteenth centuries is first clearly described by

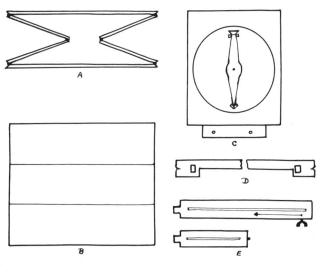

Fig. 22. An early seventeenth-century plane table; (A) frame to clamp paper to table, (B) table, (C) compass box to be attached to side of table, (D) ruler, and (E) sights. Redrawn from Hopton's *Topographicall Glasses*. (Courtesy of Library of Congress.)

Hopton. He states that the name circumferentor—"to carry about or to move on a staff"—was first used by *I. G.*, initials which, no doubt, are those of John (Iohn) Godwyn.[11] Norden had already stated that *circumferentor* was a new name given to a sort of theodolite, probably developed in central Europe during the latter half of the sixteenth century and undoubtedly derived from the compass instruments of Tartaglia, shown in Fig. 4.

Beginning with Hopton there was a tendency to divide the circular arc into 120 parts rather than into 360. It is not clear whether this method of division originated with the instrument makers or with the surveyors themselves; however, this mode of division was justified by the fact that the divisions on the circle were larger and therefore could be read more easily and with greater accuracy. At this same time there was confusion in reading the degrees cut on the compass card by the needle. On Hopton's compass card (Fig. 21*d*), 0° or 120° was at the South point of the card, while North at the point 60°. In many cases the South end of the needle was read, in other cases the North—hence there was confusion when angles of position were required.

In the actual survey Hopton is the first to use and clearly explain the method of using the general principle of triangulation, i.e., fixing points by means of two or more directed rays drawn from one or more fixed stations (Fig. 23). Although the author considers each particular problem of the survey in the light of every instrument at his disposal, his work shows the beginning of a tendency to generalize the different problems in surveying. For the first problem of measuring a piece of land he sets up one or more stations

[11] John Godwyn (fl. *ca.* 1595) was a mathematical practitioner and teacher of arithmetic and geometry in London. Hopton states that he was the inventor of the circumferentor while Rathborne speaks of his sight rule which was part of the circumferentor. Taylor, *Mathematical Practitioners*, p. 194.

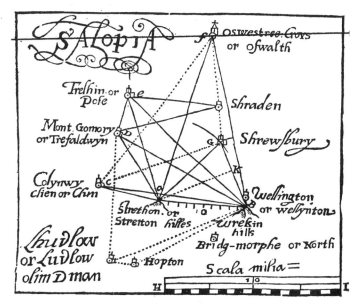

Fig. 23. A triangulation of Hopton. From Hopton's *Topo-graphicall Glasses*.
(Courtesy of the Library of Congress.)

from which he can see all the corners of the parcel of land to be surveyed. Then, with the index of the instrument, he sights the corners from the first station and reads the angle in degrees. They are read for magnitude and not for direction; hence they are read from the quadrantal divisions on the circular scale and in a clockwise direction. After all the corners have been sighted from the first station, the instrument is moved to the second station and the angles read in a similar manner. The distance between the two stations, called the *stationary line*, is used somewhat as a meridian line, and its length carefully measured so that it may be used for protraction purposes. The angles are recorded, but they are not read in such a manner that the symmetry of the plot can be obtained from the angle readings. This same method is used by Hopton to plot the location and size of an island in a river or near the coast when the distance of the island from land is not known.

In cases of large pieces of land where all the corners cannot be seen from two nearby stations, the author suggests that the surveyor locate the tops of two hills from which all the corners can be seen. He then picks a corner which lies on the East side of the North-South division of the circular instrument, and from this line as meridian he measures all the angles of the corners progressively in a clockwise direction. While measuring the angles of the corners, he frequently sights and measures the angles of important points of interest, such as houses, churches, trees, and lakes. He then moves the instrument to the second station, which may be as much as ten miles distant from the first, and measures the angle that this station makes with the East-West meridian line, taking the angles of all the points from this second station. It should be noted that the meridian line is determined by the needle of the compass.

In closing his long discussion on the field work of the survey, Hopton gives some directions for the method of survey to be used. He states that when all the corners of the land can be seen from any one corner, one should use a single station in that corner and measure all the angles and sides; when all the corners can be seen from one or more stations on the inside of the enclosure, but not from any one corner, one should then use one or two stations inside the enclosure similar to the method described above; and when the enclosure is wooded, or very large, he should use the traverse method. As for instruments, he suggests that the surveyor choose the one which he can use with the greatest ease and at the same time obtain the highest degree of accuracy. He recommends the plane table, theodolite, and topographical glasses for all ordinary types of surveying.

Hopton gives, in most cases, a full description of protracting the field notes where the lengths of the unknown sides are found by protraction. Following the method of protraction, the author makes for the first time in an English surveying text the suggestion that, when a sufficient number of sides and angles are given, trigonometry may be used in the calculation of the unknown parts of the figures. In discussing the uses of trigonometry he comments that this method is "certainly most exact and perfect in this kind of work, but that it might seem strange to young surveyors since, we have not heretofore any English Treatise showing the use of right lined Triangles" by these methods.[12]

It is apparent that Hopton has not been given the credit that he deserves. True, the logical sequence of his work is not so good as that of Rathborne and Leybourn and possibly does not surpass that of some of the writers of the early part of the century. Nevertheless, the text gives the first detailed description of the instruments used by the seventeenth-century surveyors; it shows the writer's adaptation of instruments for the particular needs of the surveyor; it provides the first detailed instructions for the use of triangulation methods of surveying; it describes the traverse methods of surveying large tracts of land; and it suggests and explains the use of trigonometry in the calculations of surveying.

To what extent Hopton's text influenced later writers of the seventeenth century it is impossible to determine. However, Aaron Rathborne and William Leybourn, two outstanding seventeenth-century writers on surveying, may have been influenced by Hopton's text.

[12] Hopton, *Topographicall Glasses*, p. 152.

Aaron Rathborne

The earliest of these two surveyors was Aaron Rath-borne,[13] who in 1616 published in London *The Surveyor in Foure Bookes*. This text is usually considered one of the most important[14] contributions to surveying in the seventeenth century. *The Surveyor* had much more of an appeal to later writers on surveying than to the average practicing surveyor of Rathborne's day. This is probably due to the fact that the text is written in a highly technical style for this age—a style which would tend to make the book appeal to the trained and educated writer on surveying more than to the practicing surveyor whose technical training in most cases was scant.

Rathborne follows the usual order of presentation. First he gives the geometry necessary for surveying, and then he describes the instruments used at this time. This is followed by a discussion of the field work and, finally, an outline of the methods of protraction and determining areas. All these topics are arranged in an orderly manner, and the definitions and discussions are treated in a clear, concise style.

Rathborne gives a much clearer description of the instruments in use during the first half of the seventeenth century than others had done. In addition, he describes his invention of a chain for measuring distances. He points out that although many instruments are in use by surveyors at this time, most surveyors use only a few of these; and he states that the theodolite (Fig. 24), plane table (Fig. 25), and the

[13] Aaron Rathborne (1572–1618) was probably a Yorkshireman. He was a prominent engraver and professional surveyor and was a member of the London group of mathematical practitioners which included Henry Briggs and John Spiedell. In 1606 he applied for a patent to engrave maps on copper, and in 1618 he was granted a patent with Roger Burgis (or Bruges) "for making a true and perfect description of London and Westminster." Taylor, *Mathematical Practitioners*, p. 191.

[14] Taylor, *Mathematical Practitioners*, pp. 58–64; 343.

Fig. 24. An illustration of Rathborne's theodolite. From Rathborne's *The Surveyor* in *Foure Bookes*.

(Courtesy of the Folger Shakespeare Library.)

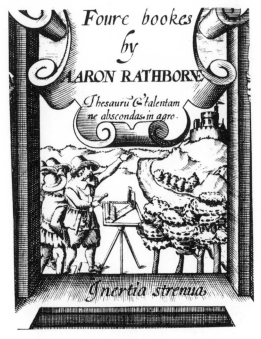

Fig. 25. An illustration of Rathborne's plane table. From Rathborne's *The Surveyor in Foure Bookes*.
(Courtesy of the Folger Shakespeare Library.)

circumferentor are sufficient for most surveying problems.
The description of the theodolite is almost that of Leonard
Digges' "topographicall instrument." (It should be noted
that Rathborne refers to the instrument as the *theodolite*,
the name by which it was called thereafter.)

Two differences were introduced into the construction of
Rathborne's theodolite. The planisphere of the theodolite
was divided into 120 parts instead of 360 degrees, and for
work on level ground a pair of sights fixed to the ruler were
attached to the planisphere (Fig. 26). The description of the

sights, which are attached to the center of the planisphere, indicates that they are double-sighted, since Rathborne states that there are two sliding vanes, "one having a slit beneath and a thread above, the other, a thread beneath, and a slit above serving to look backwards and forwards at pleasure." This is one of the earliest pairs of sights constructed for

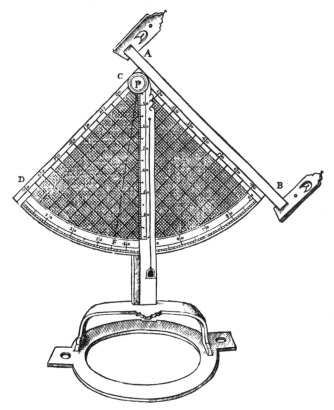

Fig. 26. The quadrant and sights used by Rathborne. From Rathborne's *The Surveyor in Foure Bookes.*
(Courtesy of the Folger Shakespeare Library.)

backsighting without turning the instrument. When the instrument is used on uneven ground, these sights and the ruler are removed and a quadrant is attached to the planisphere. Fig. 26 shows that these sights are similar to the ones described here.[15]

The first improvement in a distance-measuring instrument is shown in Rathborne's decimal chain. His description is as follows:

This is the chain before spoken of in the Peractor description; which for convenience in carriage, and auoyding casualties often happening to break it (though made of a fullround wyer) I would aduise should contain in length but only two statute Poles or Perches, or three if you please at the most. In the diuiding whereof it is to be considered, that the statute Perch or Pole, (which here we call an vnite or *Comencemente*) containeth in length 16½ feet, which is 198. ynches: This quantitye is first to be diuided into 10 equall parts called *Primes,* so shall euery of these *Primes* containe in length 19 ynches, and ⅔, of an ynch: And then these *Primes* to bee euery of them subdiuided into other 10 equall parts, which we will call *Seconds:* and so euery of these *Seconds* shall containe in length one ynch, and ⁴⁹⁄₅₀. part of an ynch. And there is the whole Perch *vnite* or comencement diuided into 100. equall parts or linckes called *Seconds.*

By those distinctions this Chaine is now diuided into three termes, *Vnites, Primes* and *Seconds,* whose Characters are these 0. 1. 2. So that you would express 26. *Vnites,* 4. *Primes,* and 5. *Seconds,* they are thus to be written 26.° 4.¹ 5.² or together thus, 2645. or briefly thus, 2645'. making prickes or points onely ouer the Fractions, whereby the rest may be conceyued to be Vnites, or Intigers, and the first point *Primes* and the next *seconds.*

This chain was a great advance over the cords and wooden poles previously used. It was a forerunner of Gunter's chain, developed a few years later, but probably did not influence Gunter in the development of his chain. It is likely, however, that both Rathborne and Gunter derived their ideas of dividing a given length into one hundred parts from

[15] Rathborne, *The Surveyor in Foure Books* (London, 1616), pp. 131–133.

Stevin's work.[16] Rathborne's decimal chain was used by many surveyors of the seventeenth century, and it is important because it not only gave the surveyor an accurate measure of length based on the statute rod or perch of 16½ feet but also allowed the easy calculation of areas with decimal fractions.

Although Rathborne's chain was a great advance over the line-measuring instruments that had been in use, a chain developed by Edmund Gunter[17] in 1620 was later used exclusively by English surveyors, and is still referred to as "Gunter's chain." Gunter's measuring instrument, which definitely involved the statute rod as a unit of land measurement, consisted of 100 links of 66 feet, with every 10 links marked off by a brass ring. A statute acre of 160 square rods measured with Gunter's chain will contain 10 square chains or 100,000 square links, and any area in square chains can easily be reduced to acres, roods, and square rods. The advantage of Gunter's chain over Rathborne's is that Gunter's could be used with either end forward, thereby lessening the possibility of error in reading parts of chains.

Gunter also developed several other devices useful in performing surveying calculations. Of these, Gunter's scale

[16] The decimal division of the surveying chain by Rathborne follows the work of Simon Stevin (1548–1620), who was the first to show by a special treatise that he understood the significance of decimal fractions. In comparing Rathborne's description of the chain with Stevin's work, *L'Arithmétique*, we see that Rathborne used Stevin's notation as well as nomenclature. Smith's *History*, Vol. 2, pp. 342–343; A. von Braunmuhl, *Vorlesungen über die Geschichte der Trigonometrie* (Leipzig, 1900), pp. 336–338; and George Sarton, "The First Explanation of Decimal Fractions and Measures (1585)," *Isis*, 23 (1938), 152–244.

[17] Edmund Gunter (1581–1626), an English astronomer, was educated at Christ College, Oxford, and was professor of astronomy at Gresham College from 1619 to 1626. He was connected with the general movement to simplify calculations in mathematics and astronomy. His complete works were published by Samuel Foster in 1662. Smith, *History*, Vol. 2; *DNB.*; Taylor, *Mathematical Practitioners*, p. 196.

or the line of numbers, the line of logarithms, and the sector were the most useful.

In the field work of the survey, Rathborne offered little in advance of Hopton's work. He divides the work under two general heads: small enclosures and large tracts of land. For surveys of the first type he discusses a case for each instrument and shows how it works. He suggests that for small enclosures the best method is to set the instrument inside the enclosure, set up some line as a meridian line, measure all angles at the corners counterclockwise from the meridian line, and finally measure the distance from the instrument to the corners. The lengths of the sides of the enclosures could then be determined by protraction or by the use of trigonometric methods.

In the case of many early surveyors, and of Rathborne in particular, it is difficult to follow the surveyor's notes and to determine just how the survey was conducted. It cannot always be determined whether the limb of any instrument is divided into 360 degrees or into 120 parts, which he calls degrees, and these divisions again divided into 60 parts, referred to as minutes. Never in the discussion does he state what manner of divisions are marked on the particular instrument being used. These difficulties are further increased by the fact that a meridian line is set up on some instruments differently from others. Also, it is not always clear which instrument has been used to obtain any given set of field notes. Furthermore, when the circumferentor is being used and the angle is determined by the needle, the instrument is turned so that the fleur-de-lis points towards the operator and thus the angle made by the South end of the needle is read.

Rathborne is careful with the protraction of his field notes. Where large tracts of land are to be measured and protracted, he usually determines many of the unknown parts by protraction, although in some cases he uses trigonometry.

The areas are determined by calculating the areas of the parts in the form of triangles or trapezia and summing the parts to find the total area. The discussion on the survey is closed with a short explanation of dividing a parcel of land so that the two parts will contain a given area.

For large tracts of land where the corners are not visible from one single point either within or without the enclosure, Rathborne uses several methods. In these he discusses each case with all the instruments at his disposal: theodolite, circumferentor, peractor, and plane table. Rathborne discusses a type of closed traverse survey somewhat different from that used by Hopton. In this survey Rathborne has the surveyor go around the enclosure, always keeping the enclosure to the right, measuring all sides and the angles formed by adjacent sides. In this type of work, however, he measures every other angle; that is, he sights from the first station A to station B, then moves his instrument directly to station C and backsights to station B, thus determining the angle ABC by backsighting. He states that this method of survey saves the operator a great amount of time.

Although earlier authors mentioned the use of some form of recording the notes of the survey in the field, Rathborne is the first English author to discuss and give a detailed description of the field book (Fig. 27):

This Booke may consist of halfe a quire of paper, to be bound (most aptly for vse) in a long Octavo: Let it be ruled towards the left margent of euery side, with four lines, so shall you describe three Collums, the first seruing for the degrees; the second (according to my Chaine) Vnites; and the third and last for Primes; or according to the accustomed vse, for degrees poles and parts of a Pole.[18]

At the close of the text Rathborne gives a lengthy discussion of the legal aspects of the survey. He points out that he is not attempting to "instruct or teach the rules or Institu-

[18] Rathborne, ref. 15, p. 156.

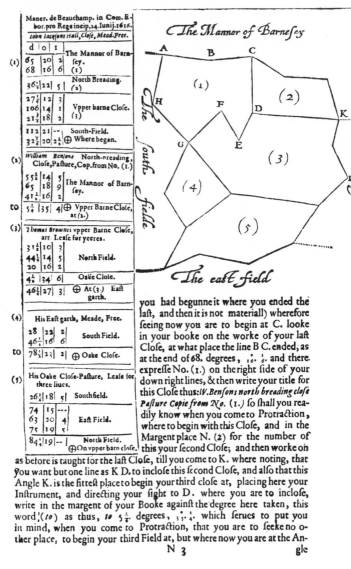

	d	o	l	
				Maner. de Beauchamp. in Com. Ebor. pro Rege incip. 24. Iunij. 1616.
				Iohn Iacksons Hall, Close, Mead. Free.
(1)	65	20	2	The Mannor of Barnsey. (1)
	68	16	6	
	$36\frac{1}{3}$	22	5	North Breading. (2)
	$27\frac{1}{4}$	12	3	Vpper barne Close. (3)
	106	14	1	
	$21\frac{1}{3}$	18	2	
	112	21	--	South-Field.
	$32\frac{3}{4}$	20	$2\frac{1}{3}$	⊕ Where began.
(2)				*William Bensons* North-breading, Close, Pasture, Cop. from No. (1.)
	$55\frac{1}{2}$	14	5	The Mannor of Barnsey.
	65	18	9	
	$41\frac{1}{2}$	16	2	
to	$5\frac{1}{4}$	35	4	⊕ Vpper Barne Close, at (2.)
(3)				*Thomas Brownes* vpper Barne Close, arr. Lease for yeeres.
	$31\frac{1}{2}$	10	3	North Field.
	$44\frac{1}{4}$	14	5	
	20	16	2	
	$4\frac{1}{6}$	34	6	Oake Close.
	$46\frac{1}{4}$	27	3	⊕ At (3.) East garth.
(4)				His East garth, Meade, Free.
	28	22	2	South Field.
	$46\frac{1}{2}$	16	6	
to	$78\frac{1}{3}$	23	2	⊕ Oake Close.
(5)				His Oake Close-Pasture, Lease for three liues.
	$26\frac{3}{4}$	18	5	Southfield.
	74	15	---	East Field.
	63	20	4	
	75	19	5	
	$84\frac{1}{4}$	19	--	North Field. ⊕ On vpper barn close.

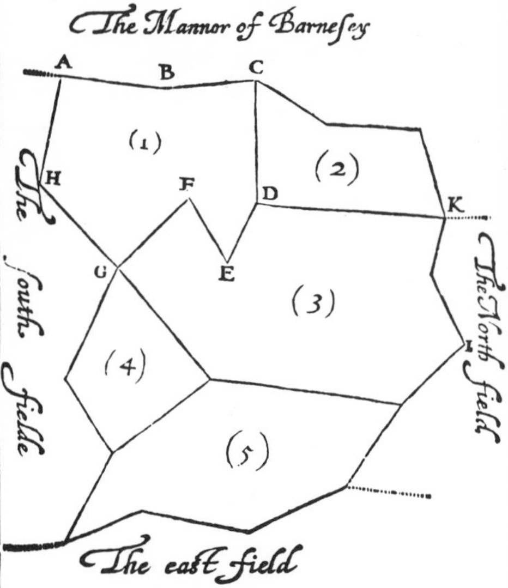

you had begunne it where you ended the last, and then it is not materiall) wherefore seeing now you are to begin at C. looke in your booke on the worke of your last Close, at what place the line B C. ended, as at the end of 68. degrees, 16. 6. and there expresse No. (1.) on the right side of your down right lines, & then write your title for this Close thus: *W. Bensons north breading close Pasture Copie from No. (1.)* so shall you readily know when you come to Protraction, where to begin with this Close, and in the Margent place N. (2) for the number of this your second Close; and then worke on as before is taught for the last Close, till you come to K. where noting, that you want but one line as K D. to inclose this second Close, and also that this Angle K. is the fittest place to begin your third close at, placing here your Instrument, and directing your sight to D. where you are to inclose, write in the margent of your Booke against the degree here taken, this word (*to*) as thus, *to* $5\frac{1}{4}$. degrees, 35. 4. which serues to put you in mind, when you come to Protraction, that you are to seeke no other place, to begin your third Field at, but where now you are at the Angle

N 3

Fig. 27. An illustration of a page from Rathborne's notebook. From Rathborne's *The Surveyor in Foure Bookes.* (Courtesy of the Folger Shakespeare Library.)

tions of the Law," but that he wishes to state briefly those principles of law that directly affect the surveyor. Rathborne then proceeds to define a manor,[19] stating in what manner "any Lands or Tenements may bee holden . . . and the several tenures dependent on these estates" with the rents and services belonging to such tenures. In careful detail he explains the rules and procedure of conducting the court, the manner of obtaining the testimony of the tenants, and the method of recording this testimony and the proceedings of the court.

Rathborne's text influenced surveyors during the seventeenth and eighteenth centuries. Not only did he improve upon existing instruments for surveying and invent the decimal chain as a line-measuring instrument, but his instructions made it possible for the surveyor to record his field notes in a systematic manner. *The Surveyor* of Rathborne remained in constant use for over a quarter of a century, until the publication of the popular text of William Leybourn in 1653.

William Leybourn

Of all the seventeenth-century writers on surveying, William Leybourn[20] probably exerted a greater influence on the practicing surveyor than any other, with the possible excep-

[19] Rathborne, ref. 15, pp. 190–228.
[20] William Leybourn (1626–1716) is usually styled a mathematician but he was also a teacher and professional land surveyor. He started his early life as a printer and probably had some connection with R. & W. Leybourn, London printers, through his whole life. He first came into notice as the coauthor, with Vincent Wing, of a book on astronomy with the title, *Urania Practica*, which is said to be the first book on astronomy written in English. In addition to the work on astronomy, Leybourn was the author of various works on surveying, arithmetic, logarithms, and mathematical recreations. The popularity of his textbooks is an indication of his ability as a textbook writer. *DNB; Smith; History,* Vol. 2, pp. 414–416; Taylor, *Mathematical Practitioners,* pp. 230–231.

tion of John Love. Leybourn's first contribution to surveying was a short pamphlet, *Pantometria or the Whole Art of
Surveying,* published in London in 1650 and written under
the pseudonym of Oliver Wallinsby. This little tract proved
so popular that Leybourn was prompted to enlarge it, and
in London in 1653 he published *The Compleat Surveyor:
Containing the Whole Art of Surveying of Land,* which
passed through four editions in the seventeenth century and
a revised edition in the first half of the eighteenth century.

Leybourn's texts are written in a clear, attractive style
which probably developed out of his extensive teaching
experience. They are a decided improvement over most of
the texts published previously: the material is better organized, and there is a definite trend toward a generalization
of the different methods of surveying. Although this trend
was noticeable in Aaron Rathborne's *The Surveyor,* it is
much more decided in Leybourn's writings.

In the preface to *The Compleat Surveyor,* Leybourn
states that he has drawn from many sources; in particular,
the geometrical definitions are taken from Euclid, Ramus,
and Clavius, while the trigonometric solutions of problems
are drawn from Pitiscus, Snell, Gunter, and Norwood. Leybourn seems to be the first surveyor to give an extensive
discussion of the use of logarithms and trigonometry in casting up the areas of the survey.

In his description of instruments Leybourn discusses only
a few in detail, such as the theodolite, the circumferentor,
and the plane table. This would indicate that the number
of instruments being used was decreasing; there was a tendency to rely upon and to improve a few of the instruments
and to use these few for the purpose to which they were
best adapted. Leybourn proposes to use the theodolite and
circumferentor for large surveys, whereas the plane table
will be used for small surveys and enclosures. His descriptions of the theodolite and circumferentor are quite similar

to those of Hopton and Rathborne. Leybourn states, however, that the geometrical square constructed within the
horizontal circle of the theodolite is seldom used and that
it could be easily dispensed with.

He suggests several changes in the plane table. The clamps
are to be attached so that the paper will be held more
securely on the frame. One side of the frame is divided into
equal parts similar to the divisions on the side of Rathborne's
plane table, whereas on the other side Leybourn adds the
divisions of the semicircle, thus making it possible to use the
plane table as a sort of circumferentor. The second major
change in the plane table involves the sights. He constructs
both sights of the same length; and instead of a single slit
in both sights, he has a small, round hole at the top and a slit
at the bottom of one, and a slit at the top and a round hole
at the bottom of the other, thereby facilitating the use of
the two sights for backsighting as well as foresighting. Leybourn then discusses several instruments of minor importance, the most useful of which was the cross, somewhat
similar to the Roman Groma, for taking offsets. In the discussion of line-measuring instruments Leybourn mentions
the chains of Rathborne and Gunter as being the most satisfactory and the ones that are generally used.

In the field work Leybourn does not differ essentially
from Hopton and Rathborne. The Prologue to the fourth
book, in which the field work is discussed, states that "every
kind of work is performed three separate ways, by the
several Instruments"; that is, by the plane table, the theodolite, and the circumferentor. This statement in the Prologue
is in reality not carried out, since the author actually considers five different methods of surveys with the three instruments, as well as the method of surveying with the chain
only and the survey of a large tract of land with the circumferentor by measuring the sides and the bearing angles. The
five cases of surveying are adequately illustrated in Fig. 28.

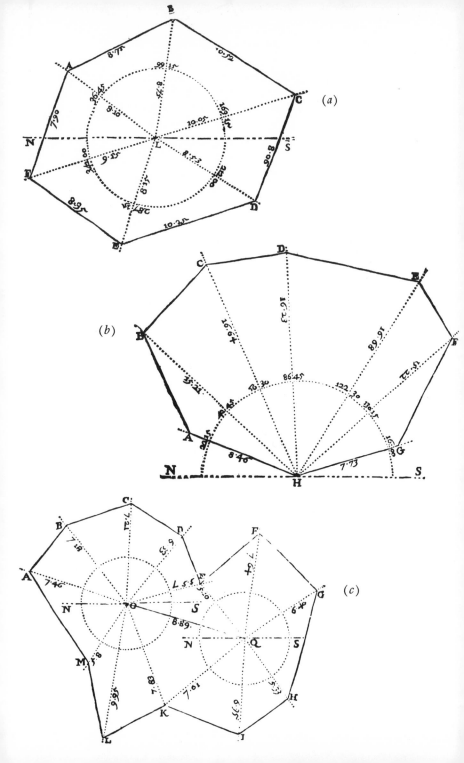

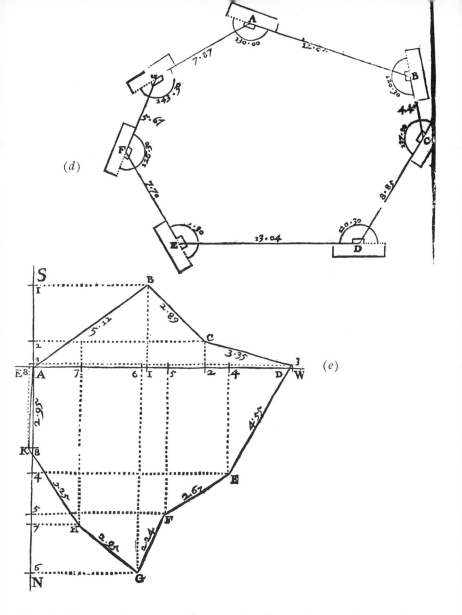

Fig. 28. Diagrams illustrating the methods of surveying used
by Leybourn;
    (a) one station inside the enclosure,
    (b) one station at a corner of the enclosure,
    (c) two stations inside the enclosure,
    (d) traversing the perimeter with the plane table, and
    (e) traversing the perimeter with the circumferentor.
    From Leybourn's *The Compleat Surveyor*.
(Courtesy of the University of Columbia Libraries.)

There is only a slight difference between Leybourn's method of protraction and casting up the area and those of Rathborne and other surveyors of the seventeenth century. We do note, however, that Leybourn is more explicit in his directions for these operations than previous writers. He points out the advantages of the use of Rathborne's decimal chain in the calculations of area and mentions the ease of converting customary acres to statute acres.

The Compleat Surveyor of Leybourn added little new to surveying. Nevertheless, the clear style and simplicity with which the subject was presented greatly influenced the practicing surveyor of the second half of the seventeenth century.

John Eyre

Within one year after the publication of Leybourn's *The Compleat Surveyor*, John Eyre published *The Exact Surveyor*.[21] This work was probably not influenced by Leybourn's work, but may have been by that of Rathborne, since the descriptions of instruments are almost identical with those of the latter. The work is a lucid discussion of the art of surveying written in clear style, but it hardly reaches the high degree of perfection of Rathborne and Leybourn.

The organization of Eyre's book is somewhat different from those of previously published texts. In the first place, the description of instruments is given early in the text, before the brief section on geometry. Another feature is the table of logarithms of sines of angles and numbers and their application to the solution of the parts of triangles. The author also gives methods for the use of logarithms in the

[21] John Eyre, *The Exact Surveyor* (London, 1654). Eyre (fl. *ca.* 1654) is described by Taylor as a practitioner in mathematics. He wrote a textbook on surveying and we are probably correct in assuming that he practiced the art of surveying. Taylor, *Mathematical Practitioners*, p. 241.

calculations following the survey. He makes an attempt at a generalization of formulas and methods of survey followed by some crude checks on the work of the surveyor in the field.

Although Eyre is the first seventeenth-century author to make an attempt at a comprehensive discussion of the errors in the survey, he does not go beyond the simplest checks of geometry and trigonometry that had been given in a disconnected form by other surveyors. He first gives the familiar formula for the sum of the angles of a polygon: the sum of the angles is equal to $180 \ (n-2)$, where n is the number of sides of the polygon. Then he discusses in detail closure when the bearing of the angles of closed traverse is taken of the enclosure. If the sum of the eastings equals the sum of the westings and the sum of the northings equals the sum of the southings, "you may be assured that youre worke is exact. But if there be much difference, you must correct your plot by more circumspect observations of the sides, and their Angles." Although his discussion of closure is lengthy, the author nevertheless fails to give any limit to the lack of closure, nor does he give any suggestion for its correction except to resurvey the part or parts which seem to be in error.[22]

In the calculation of areas and protraction of the parts of the survey, Eyre follows closely the methods of Rathborne and Leybourn. He does, however, lay more stress on the use of logarithms and on trigonometric methods than any previous author, stating that the parts of a triangle can usually be more advantageously computed by the aid of logarithms and trigonometry than by any other method. Eyre also attempts, in a small way, to bring to the attention of the surveyor some of the errors inherent in his work and proposes several ineffective methods for their correction.

[22] Eyre, *op. cit.*, pp. 118–122.

A study of the errors of surveying was again considered in the work of George Atwell which followed in 1568.

George Atwell

In 1658 George Atwell published *The Faithful Surveyor*,[23] which was the first text of the seventeenth century to attempt to show that land surveying could be done as accurately, and at the same time more quickly, by the chain alone as by any single-angle measuring instrument. In the preface the author mentions that the manuscript had been read and criticized by several teachers at Cambridge, none of whom, however, was a surveyor. He asserts that he is writing to two groups of readers: the scholar who may be interested in this subject for the sake of the subject itself, and the honest country farmer, in order that he may be able to measure his own lands.

The text as a whole contains little of the arithmetic and geometry given by contemporary writers. On the contrary, Atwell begins his discussion by pointing out two of the most common of the serious errors committed by land surveyors: (1) they regard the areas of two pieces of land as proportional to their perimeters, and (2) many of them use the incorrect form of the areas of a triangle as the product of one half the base multiplied by the length of the line drawn from the opposite vertex to the midpoint of the base. Atwell then states that the professional surveyor, Balls of London, surveyed a piece of land and gave the content

[23] George Atwell, *The Faithful Surveyor* (London, 1658). Atwell (1588–1659) was a surveyor, instructor, and writer on surveying. His name is given on the title page of the *Faithful Surveyor* as George Atwell, alias Wells. He designed and constructed his own instruments and was friendly with some of the best-known instrument makers of the period. John le Neve, *Monumenta Anglicana* (London, 1719), Vol. 2, p. 48; Taylor, *Mathematical Practitioners*, p. 199.

as 400 acres, and that he later surveyed the same land and found the content to be 322 acres, revealing a discrepancy of approximately 25 per cent of the correct area. Atwell also points out that since this same land was being rented for five shillings an acre each year for a term of twenty-one years, the necessity of making accurate surveys of land is obvious. He further gives some of the "uncertain ways" of surveying; that is, putting too large a plot on too small a piece of paper, relying too much on the graduated scale of the compass card in reading the needle, being overcautious and consuming too much time in the survey, and using the methods of logarithms and trigonometry to determine the areas of triangles. He reminds the reader that the time and care with which a surveyor does his work should depend to a great extent on the value of the land and that a good surveyor should earn about one-half pound for his day's work.

In the field work of the survey Atwell prefers the chain or plane table to any other instrument; he does not consider as many different cases or problems in the survey as the earlier writers, and he generally gives more attention to offsets than the writers who have preceded him. He is one of the first writers on surveying to give detailed instructions with respect to the boundaries of the survey.

Atwell is specific and careful with his protraction; for example, when the survey has been done by the plane table he suggests that the protraction should be replotted from the field notes. He cautions against the use of too small a scale and states that the plot should close with an error of not more than one pole, but in giving this rule he does not take into consideration the size of the enclosure.

Atwell's contribution to surveying is the continued recognition of the errors arising in the surveying of land. Although there are few suggestions for their correction, nevertheless the surveyor is urged to perform the field work with the greatest of care and thereby reduce the number of errors to a minimum.

Vincent Wing

Within six years after Atwell's text, the work of Vincent Wing[24] offered a somewhat different approach to the subject of surveying. Wing's *The Geodaetes Practicus: or The Art of Surveying*, published in London in 1664, is of considerable interest, for it is probably the first work on surveying to be written for use as a handbook. There is a slight possibility that this work is in some way connected with the surveying works of William Leybourn, since we have already seen that Wing and Leybourn collaborated in writing the *Urania Practica* (see Footnote 20), a short work on astronomy. Furthermore the parts of the text dealing specifically with surveying follow the same general line as Leybourn's *Compleat Surveyor;* this is particularly true of the description of instruments and the field work of the survey.

Wing is careful in the protraction of the field notes and discusses in detail the construction of a scale of equal parts to be used when the measurements are done with Gunter's chain. Accuracy of the protraction is essential, since many of the distances are determined by protraction and are then to be used in determining the areas of the figures. Many surveyors do not pay enough attention to the accuracy of

[24] Vincent Wing (1619–1668) was self-educated and is usually styled as an astronomer. He wrote several works on astronomy and from 1640 to 1660 he issued the ephemerides as well as a number of almanacs. He also conducted numerous surveying expeditions during this period. *DNB.;* John Gadbury, *Brief Relation of the Life and Death of Vincent Wing* (London, 1669); Granger, *Biographical History of England* (London); and Taylor, *Mathematical Practitioners,* p. 300.

their calculations, he claims, for in resurveys of areas ranging from 500 to 1,000 acres, he has found errors as great as 100 acres in the calculations.

In calculating areas, Wing uses the same methods as Rathborne and Leybourn. He does, however, make considerable use of trigonometry and logarithms in his calculations and consequently does not depend entirely upon protraction for the determination of auxiliary lines. In addition to the usual methods of computing areas, he suggests a novel method by protracting a given known area on a piece of paper, then carefully cutting out this drawing along the borders and weighing the paper, thereby obtaining the weight of paper for the unit of area used. When a large enclosure has been protracted with the same scale on paper of like thickness, the area of the enclosure can be determined by weighing the large sheet of paper and comparing this weight with the weight of the unit area. This method had been previously used in 1598.

Vincent Wing gave to the practicing surveyor a small, handy book on surveying which could be carried for reference while executing the field work of the survey. He insisted upon a high degree of accuracy in his calculations and discussed surveying by the chain only to a greater extent than others had done.

Adam Martindale

Wing's method of surveying by the chain only was explained and used with greater frequency by Adam Martindale, a schoolteacher, professional surveyor, and clergyman, who wrote a number of textbooks on arithmetic and who published *The Country-Survey-Book* in 1682.[25] This text

[25] Adam Martindale, *The Country-Survey-Book: or Land-Meter's Vademecum* (London, 1682). (Hereafter referred to as *Country-Sur-*

was apparently popular and widely used by surveyors, passing through eleven editions or reprintings.

In his preface the author states that the country abounds with men who would like to do a better job of surveying, but there is a lack of good, inexpensive texts describing in simple terms surveying methods and the use of practical, inexpensive instruments. Martindale points out that there are a number of excellent works on the subject, mentioning those of Rathborne, Leybourn, and Atwell, which he believes are too complicated for the beginner. He proposes to write a small, inexpensive book with the necessary geometrical parts and a simple explanation of the theory of surveying for the beginner or for anyone who wishes to extend his knowledge of surveying. This section is interesting in that it gives an idea of the method used—by an experienced teacher—for instructing young men in the profession of surveying. Martindale suggests that the student should first study and master the geometrical principles and demonstrations which would be required in surveying; then the student should take "a small Packthread and by knots about half Inch asunder divide it into 100 parts, as Gunter's chain is divided."[26] With this thread as a chain the student would be able to measure all sorts and shapes of figures in his study and then would be able to plot these figures on paper.

In the field work Martindale follows closely the methods used by the leading surveyors and land measurers of the seventeenth century. He discusses the uses of all instruments

---

vey.) Martindale (1623–1686) was a nonconformist clergyman and teacher. He joined the Parliamentary forces during the English Civil War. After the passing of the Conventicle Acts he was forced to give up teaching in the free schools and from then till his death he taught students privately. Taylor, *Mathematical Practitioners*, p. 226.

[26] Martindale, *Country-Survey*, Preface A₂.

but prefers the plane table and Gunter's chain in the survey. This discussion is followed by general instructions for the practicing surveyor similar to those given earlier by Atwell. These instructions, though simple, are important, since in modified form they were passed on as rules by the land office in the manuals for practicing surveyors. The more important rules given by Martindale are

1. If there is a previous agreement regarding the boundary, this agreement must be followed throughout the survey; if there is no agreement, then the surveyor must use reason and follow the prevailing customs.
2. Commons are usually measured to the utmost bounds of every man's particular proportion without making allowances for ditches and fences.
3. The boundaries between lord and tenant, in case of a lease for life or long tenure, is carried to the utmost bounds of the tenant's claims and is to include walls, hedges, and ditches. This rule, according to the author, frequently causes dissatisfaction, but he states that this is the custom and where custom obtains, the surveyor must observe it "for it is others' work to appoint what must be measured, and is only to measure truly what is so appointed."
4. Where land is measured for sale at a given rate per acre, no boundaries being agreed upon, the lines extend to the quick-wood-row or where by reason it should grow or be set.

The author states that these rules may seem trivial; but, unless followed, mistakes in practice, misunderstandings, and litigation may result. [27]

Martindale is an exponent of surveying exclusively with the chain, since he asserts that the majority of the errors of

[27] Martindale, *Country-Survey*, pp. 122–124.

surveying are due to the use of angle-measuring instruments. Use of the chain as the principal instrument for surveys reduced the cost of equipment to a minimum and lowered the time required to complete the survey. This method of surveying was carried into the eighteenth century, as *surveying with the long lines,* and was greatly favored by several prominent surveyors.

Martindale's *Country-Survey* gives us an insight into the poor instruction given to young surveyors during the last half of the seventeenth century. It also indicates the beginning of a trend back to the method of surveying with the chain.

John Love

The last important writer on surveying of the seventeenth century was John Love, who published in 1688 a book with the title, *Geodaesia.*[28] Love states that he was impelled to write a treatise on surveying by a desire to help young surveyors in America, whom he had seen trying to lay out lands when their books would not give them any aid in their work, and further that he wished to give new methods of mapping and making soundings of the entrances to rivers and harbors. The book was apparently popular and was well received, since it passed through at least eleven editions of printings in England between 1688 and 1792, and two editions, the twelfth and thirteenth, were published in the United States in 1793 and 1796.

[28] John Love, *Geodaesia: or the Art of Surveying and Measuring of Land Made Easie* (London, 1688). Love (fl. 1688–1711) styled himself as "Philomathematicus." Little is known of his early life, but he was a surveyor in North Carolina and Jamaica before returning to England to write his surveying text. The twelfth and thirteenth editions of this text seem to have been the earliest English texts on surveying reprinted in the United States. Louis Karpinski, *Bibliography of Mathematical Works Printed in America Through 1850* (Ann Arbor, 1940), p. 10; Taylor, *Mathematical Practitioners,* p. 284.

Love gives more detailed information on the actual survey than any previous writer. His methods are similar to those of Rathborne, Leybourn, Wing, and others, but he brings to the work a refinement of method which gives a much higher degree of accuracy and simplicity than had been attained by others. Moreover, throughout the text he shows where generalizations in methods could be made, and to a certain extent he simplifies the whole process of land surveying. His first step in discussing the survey is to explain that there are two general problems of surveying in the field: first, the measurement of distances; second, the measurement of angles. For the measurement of distances he discusses the use of both Rathborne's and Gunter's chains but seems to use Gunter's exclusively in his work. There are almost as many instruments for the measurement of angles as there are surveyors, Love asserts. However, he points out that of all these, the plane table, circumferentor, theodolite, and semi-circle are the ones in most esteem. In recording the field notes he cautions that the surveyor should use care.

In discussing the various surveying instruments he points out some of their advantages and disadvantages. For example, in discussing the circumferentor he states that the needle is used exclusively, and as a consequence the instrument is not satisfactory for use near iron ore deposits. In America, however, where there are thick woods, it is probably the best instrument for the survey. Love asserts that if the operator points the fleur-de-lis toward the object, the angle cut by the North end of the needle should be read, but if the fleur-de-lis is pointed toward the operator, the angle cut by the South end of the needle should be read. If the compass card is divided into quadrants, the fleur-de-lis should always be pointed away from the operator. Love believes that dividing the compass card into four 90° quadrants is the most satisfactory. He also points out that the method of taking the bearing angle is the simplest and most accurate, since instead of reading the angle between two lines, it is only necessary to take the angle that each line makes with the North-South meridian.

Love gives complete directions for surveying various types of enclosures with the instruments at his disposal, using methods of survey similar to those used by Leybourn and illustrated in Fig. 28. These different problems are sometimes undertaken with one instrument and sometimes with more than one. In surveying woods and other similar areas, as well as large tracts of land, particularly in America, Love recommends the use of the circumferentor, giving the bearings of the courses and then measuring the lengths. In this method the instrument is set at each corner, observing the bearings of the courses and then measuring their lengths. The operator should write his readings in the form "*AB, NW*. 7°, 28 chains, 20 links." This is the most desirable manner from which to plot the field notes, he claims, and states that it is the method used by most surveyors in America where large tracts of land have been surveyed. Another advantage of this method is in testing the accuracy of the survey by checking the closure; that is, by comparing the sum of the eastings with the sum of the westings and the sum of the northings with the sum of the southings. The northings and southings are the differences in latitude and the eastings and westings are the differences in longitude.

Like most of the earlier surveyors, Love was careful about the protraction of the results of the survey. The method of protraction is used to some extent, but not exclusively, for determining the length of sides of figures. Love is more inclined to use the plot or map in its true sense as a map of the tract of land. He attempts to indicate the positions and nearly always gives the directions so that there will be no difficulty in locating points or places on the map or plot. When the protractor, rather than the line of chords, is used for plotting angles, the paper is divided by means of parallel lines, the top of the sheet is used for North, the bottom for South, the right-hand side for East, and the left-hand side for West. In this case the North-South meridian line is shown by means of a compass drawing.

In determining areas he first discusses measures in general, defining the units of length and showing the relation of one to another. He then explains the differences between the chains in use and how to find the area with Gunter's chain. Computation of the area is usually done by dividing the figure into triangles, generally without the use of trigonometry. With hills and valleys Love suggests that special care must be taken, since the "superficial area" is computed, whereas for the purpose of plotting, the plan figure is needed.

The *Geodaesia* of Love is significant in that it is a clear, concise exposition of the description of instruments and methods of surveying. Although many of these topics had been discussed by others, Love gives the most complete directions for the actual survey. The rules and procedures are well defined, and his directions are clear and simple. Furthermore, Love is the first English writer to consider the surveying of land in America where the conditions under which the field work was conducted differed from those in England.

Love's text was the last reported English work on surveying of the seventeenth century. In addition to the significant texts and handbooks on surveying, developments in mathematical instruments during the century had a tremendous impact on the construction of surveying instruments and the progress of surveying in the eighteenth century.

Mathematical Instruments: The Vernier

In reviewing the progress in instrument construction, we should not neglect several major inventions and advances during the seventeenth century which, although not used to any great extent at the time they were developed, had a profound influence on instrument construction during the following century. One important invention was in the method of dividing or reading linear and circular scale divisions, an invention known as the "vernier" but frequently given the misnomer of "nonius."

The history of the vernier is somewhat complicated by the fact that the principle of the vernier was suggested to Tycho Brahe by Jacques Curtius in 1590, although there is little or no evidence that the idea was put into practical operation before Pierre Vernier took it into hand in 1631. In that year Vernier published a paper describing the invention and explaining its application to a quadrant of a circle.[29] Although this invention was completed and a description published in 1631, its application and use for reading graduations on a scale was not applied to surveying instruments for almost a century.

The Telescope

A second invention of the seventeenth century that was destined to change the surveying instruments of the eighteenth century was the telescope. Although there are claims that the telescope was invented before the seventeenth century (by Roger Bacon about 1270, Porta about 1558, and Leonard Digges about 1571), there is no definite evidence to support any claims prior to 1608. Historians have credited

[29] Pierre Vernier, *La construction, l'usage et les propriétés de quadrant nouveau de mathématique* (Brussels, 1631).

the invention of the telescope to Jan Lippershey, a spectacle-maker and lens grinder of Middleburgh. A rival claim was set up by Zacarius Jansen, another spectaclemaker, but the official documents at the Hague show that those of Lippershey were earlier by a few days and were supported by the award of money on 2 October 1608, by the States General.[30] However, recent research has shown that the priority of the invention of the telescope by Lippershey and Jansen may have been preceded by similar work in Italy, the main center of optical study.[31]

The telescope developed by Lippershey had a close resemblance to the first compound microscopes in that it consisted of a combination of a double convex lens as object glass and a double concave lens as eyepiece. This instrument is still referred to as the "Dutch type" of telescope. The news of the discovery seems to have reached Galileo Galilei in 1609[32]; and he applied all his energies and superior knowledge of optics to the construction of a telescope that could be used for astronomical work. His efforts, as could be expected, surpassed those of the Dutch spectaclemakers, and by 1610 he had published in his *Sidereus Nuncius* a description of a telescope that he had developed for use in astronomical work.

[30] Louis Bell, *The Telescope* (New York, 1922), pp. 1–30.
[31] L. M. Angus-Butterworth, "Lenses and Optical Instruments," *History of Technology*, Charles Singer *et al.*, ed. (Oxford, 1958), Vol. 3, pp. 229–233.
[32] Galileo Galilei (1564–1642) first studied medicine at the University of Pisa but became interested in geometry and later devoted his entire time to mathematics and the physical sciences. He was professor of mathematics at the University of Padua when he worked on the telescope and invented his proportional compasses. Galileo was one of the most brilliant and at the same time one of the most controversial figures of the century. Smith; *History*, Vol. 1; and Giorgio de Santillana, *The Crime of Galileo* (Chicago, 1955).

In 1611 Johannes Kepler[33] explained the fundamental principles of the Dutch or Galilean type of telescope and suggested certain definite changes in its construction. These changes consisted primarily of using two convergent lenses so placed that the object glass was at such a distance from the object that the image was blurred and indistinct, and then placing a second convergent lens between the eye and the blurred image, making the image larger and distinct. Telescopes of this type are usually referred to as astronomical or Keplerian telescopes. Such a telescope was never constructed by Kepler, but from his suggestions—with slight modifications—a telescope of this type was constructed some time between 1613 and 1617 by the Jesuit Christoph Scheiner.[34]

The Micrometer

The astronomical, or Keplerian, telescope had important advantages over the Dutch type. Its wider field of vision, which made possible the comparison of the image of a distant object with some small object placed in the common focus of the two lenses, led to the development in 1638 of the micrometer of William Gascoigne.[35] Although Gas-

[33] Kepler (1571–1630) is known chiefly for his work in astronomy but is usually ranked highly by English writers as a mathematician. He worked under Tycho Brahe and became court astronomer in 1601 to Emperor Rudolph II. Smith, *History*, Vol. 1.

[34] On the history of the development of the telescope see: A. Wolf, *A History of Science, Technology, and Philosophy in the 16th and 17th Centuries* (New York, 1939), pp. 75–82; T. Court and M. von Rohr, "A History of the Telescope," *Transactions of the Optical Society*, 30 (1929), 207–260; 32 (1931), 113–122.

[35] William Gascoigne (1612–1644) was a self-taught mathematician. After studying and practicing Oughtred's *Clavius*, he discovered his talent for constructing and improving instruments for observational work. He joined the Royalist forces in the English Civil Wars and was killed at the Battle of Marston Moor. He left a completed manu-

coigne's invention seems to have been forgotten for almost twenty years, it has been definitely established that he not only invented but used the micrometer in astronomical work before he died. His instrument consisted of either two parallel wires or two parallel plates of metal placed in the focus of the eyepiece of the telescope and capable of being moved so that the image of an object could be compressed between the two plates or wires. These plates or wires were moved by a very finely divided screw arrangement which had a scale attached, so that the distance between the plates or wires could be read very accurately. Gascoigne used this instrument to measure the angles between two objects and also to measure the relative diameters of the moon and planets. He was probably the first to attach the telescope with his micrometer arrangement to a quadrant and to use it in astronomical work.[36]

Gascoigne's invention was forgotten until a letter from Adrian Auzout (*ca.* 1640–1691) to Henry Oldenberg (1615–1677), Secretary of the Royal Society of London, announced the development of the micrometer by himself and Jean Picard (1620–1682), both astronomers at the Paris Observatory. This letter was inserted in the twenty-first number of the *Philosophical Transactions*, and a description of the Auzout and Picard micrometer was published in 1773.[37] When this letter was presented to the Royal Society, several members stated that methods of reading small angles were already known in England. Several letters from Gascoigne to his friend Crabtree, which were later deposited with

script on optics which was never published. *DNB;* and *Taylor, Mathematical Practitioners,* p. 216.

[36] Robert Grant, *History of Physical Astronomy* (London, 1852), pp. 450–455.

[37] Adrian Auzout, "Manière Exacte Pour Prendre le Diamètre des Planètes," *Histoire de l'Académie Royale des Sciences depuis 1666 jusqu'à 1699* (Paris, 1773), Vol. 3, pp. 118–130.

Richard Townley, were presented to the Society.[38] One, dated 25 January 1640, described the micrometer and stated that it might be applied to a sextant; another letter, dated 22 December 1641, gave a description of the wheels and screws of the micrometer of Gascoigne. A reproduction of Gascoigne's micrometer was constructed by Robert Hooke (1635–1703) and exhibited before the Royal Society at a meeting held on 25 July 1667, and a detailed description was subsequently given in Volume 29 of the *Philosophical Transactions*.

The evidence is conclusive that Gascoigne invented and used the micrometer with metal plates about 1640 and that Auzout and Picard developed the micrometer using human hair, without knowledge of the previous invention of Gascoigne. The French astronomer Morin unsuccessfully attempted to use telescopic sights as early as 1635, but Picard, about 1667, was probably the first to use the telescope in relation to a surveying instrument, whereas the early application of telescopic sights to astronomical instruments was usually to the sextant or quadrant. Hevelius had used the method of the vernier of Peter Vernier in 1631; this was later modified by Øle Römer in 1690, in such a manner that a transit circle and an altazimuth circle could be used.[39]

[38] W. Derham, "Extract from Mr. Gascoigne and Mr. Crabtrie Letters; Proving Mr. Gascoigne to have been the Inventor of Telescopic Sights of Mathematical Instruments, and not the French," *Philosophical Transactions of the Royal Society of London, 30* (1717), pp. 603–610.

[39] For a complete discussion of the use of the telescope as applied to astronomical and surveying instruments, see: Charles S. Howe, "Early History of Instruments and the Art of Observing in Astronomy and Civil Engineering," *Journal of Associated Engineering Societies, 18* (1897), 170 ff; F. L. E. Dreyer, "On the Invention of the Sextant," *Astronomische Nachrichten, 115* (1886), 31–35; and the *Catalogue of the Collection of the Science Museum of South Kensington—Geodesy and Surveying*, compiled by E. Lancaster-Jones (London, 1925), pp. 50–55.

The Stadia

The introduction of cross hairs into the focal plane of the object glass of the telescope, in particular those cross hairs intersecting at right angles, added to the possibilities of the instrument. Not only was this scheme useful in fixing the line of sight on the distant object, but it made possible the development of another form of the instrument, known as the stadia. Although not used until nearly a century later, the stadia was definitely developed by 1664.

The Italian physicist and astronomer Geminiano Montanari (1633–1687)[40] was almost certainly the first to conceive the idea of measuring distances by means of the parallel rulings in the focal plane of the telescope. His method was to place two or more threads parallel to each other and then to read the distance on a graduated rod set up perpendicular to the line of sight and at a reasonable distance from the telescope. After determining the standard for the particular position of the hairs in the telescope or instrument, it was possible to determine any distance from the scale reading on the rod. This use of the telescope was not rediscovered until the latter part of the eighteenth century.

Levels: Leveling

Leveling in the seventeenth century was done by instruments which, for the most part, used the fundamental principles of the ancients. In order to set the plane of his instruments level with the horizontal, the surveyor still used some form of the plumb bob, except in a few cases in the early part of the century where a long needle was used. In many cases the line or the plumb bob was made to cut a

[40] Angelo Salmoiraghi, *Istrumenti e Metodi Moderni di Geometria Applicata* (Milano, 1884), Vol. I, Part I, pp. 278–279.

number of divisions on a scale which was usually on a quadrant or semicircle. Levels of this type were probably used for short distances in order to determine the slope of a line for the conduction of water or for use with artillery. In addition to these levels, a number of water levels were developed in the seventeenth century. Some followed the chorobates type of Vitruvius, while others were of a slightly advanced design. According to La Hire,[41] a device was developed by Riccioli in which the level of the liquid rose to a definite height in two turned-up ends of a glass tube. This form of level continued in use for almost two centuries, although the spirit bubble level was developed shortly after the Riccioli type of level gained its popularity.

Credit for the invention of the important spirit level, making use of the bubble, is usually ascribed to Melchisédech Thevénot. This invention was made public in an anonymous tract, now credited to Thevénot, published in Paris in 1666. A second description by Thevénot appeared in 1681 in a short treatise on navigation.[42] The description of the level is simple. The author states that a glass tube, with parallel sides and a diameter about the size of the little finger, was sealed at one end. A length was then taken about seven or eight times the inside diameter of the tube, which portion was then almost filled with spirits and the other end of the tube sealed. The author points out that the unfilled space left in the tube should give a bubble whose length would be approximately the diameter of the tube. He then goes on to explain that when the tube was in a horizontal position, a mark was cut on the glass tube across the center of the longitudinal axis of the bubble. After this center had been cut, two or three other lines were cut on both sides of this

[41] Philip de la Hire, *L'Ecole des Arpentures* (Paris, 1689), pp. 146–150.

[42] Melchisédech Thevénot, *Machine Nouvelle Pour Conduire les Eaux* (Paris, 1666) and his *Discours sur l'Art de la Navigation* (Paris, 1681), pp. 10–11.

center line so that when the tube was attached to a staff the amount of elevation or depression could be measured. However, it is not clear from the context the exact scale used for these divisions.

The bubble spirit level was slow in coming into common use on the Continent as well as in England, and there is considerable confusion regarding its development.[43] The tardiness in its acceptance was no doubt due to the mechanical difficulties in the construction of the containing tube, a difficulty not overcome until accurate construction of curved tubes was accomplished. In England various forms of levels were used throughout the seventeenth century. There are many examples of plumb-bob levels in the Science Museum at Kensington and in other collections of instruments; however, the water level in some form seems to have been in particularly great demand during the latter half of the seventeenth century.

That the bubble level was slow in being used for practical surveying is probably best shown by three references from Leybourn's texts on surveying. In the first he states, "There is an Instrument called the water-level, for the performance hereof the making is sufficiently known." From the diagram given in the text it is impossible to determine the exact type of instrument referred to, but in the fourth edition the reference was expanded, giving a definite clue to the type of level used: "They are usually made about 5 or 6 Foot long, having a trough cover'd over, or a Copper Pipe to hold the water, and two cups, at each End one into which the water must issue to set the Level truly."[44] This statement makes it clear that the type of level generally used by surveyors at the time of the publication of the first edition

---

[43] Thomas Stevenson, "Some Account of Leveling Instruments," *Journal of the Franklin Institute, 8,* 3rd ser. (1884), 217 ff.

[44] Leybourn, *The Compleat Surveyor,* 1st ed. (London, 1657), pp. 305–307.

of the *Compleat Surveyor* was a modified type of the chorobates level.

Following this reference is a description of another type of level which is apparently some form of spirit level. From the statement given by Leybourn, however, this level had not come into general use in 1679, the date of publication of the fourth edition.[45] In the revised fifth edition of the *Compleat Surveyor,* published in 1727, we are told how levels were made at that time, possibly similar to Fig. 29:

> Water-Levels now a days are generally made with Spirits enclosed either in a Glass Tube or a circular flat Box, Cover'd with a Glass Cover, ground Convex, fix'd to a Telescope with Horizontal Hairs, in such manner, that if the bubble be brought to the mark on the Glass, the hairs are Horizontal.[46]

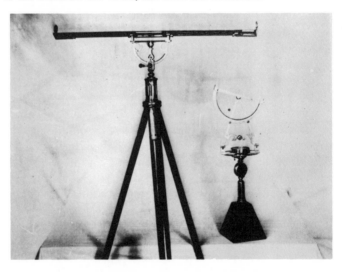

Fig. 29. Rowley's bubble level, about 1704. Photograph from the Collection, Whipple Science Museum, Cambridge. (Courtesy of the Curator.)

[45] Leybourn, *op. cit.,* 4th ed. (London, 1679), pp. 125–126.
[46] Leybourn, *op. cit.,* 5th ed. (London, 1727), pp. 122–123.

This statement indicates that the level by the first quarter of the eighteenth century had reached a high degree of perfection and was probably of the type used by Sisson (explained in Chapter 6).

Summary of Seventeenth-Century Developments

By the close of the seventeenth century, a number of advances had been made in surveying, not only in the methods of survey but also in the instruments used. Among those who advanced the profession were John Norden, Arthur Hopton, and Aaron Rathborne. Norden tried to reconcile the differences between surveyor and tenant, showing that the surveyor was as much a friend of the tenant as of the landlord or lord of the manor. He also introduced the circumferentor into English surveying practice and was probably one of the first English surveyors to use backsighting in his field practice. Hopton, on the other hand, was the first to give a detailed description of all the important surveying instruments in use in England.

Hopton used the diagonal method of division of his instruments, thus making it possible to obtain more accurate reading of the angles; he gave the first description of the tripod as a support for the instruments; he was the first English writer to suggest the use of the traverse method of survey; and he used triangulation to a much greater extent than had been previously done by any surveyor of whom anything is known. Hopton also suggested the use of trigonometry in his computations and directed the attention of the surveyor to the need for careful and accurate protracting.

A few years later Rathborne elaborated on the work that Hopton had begun and then gave us his field book and the decimal chain. This was followed somewhat later by the chain of Edmund Gunter, which played a decisive part in the adoption of the standard rod of 16½ feet in length measurements.

The surveyors of the second half of the seventeenth century continued to progress. In particular, Leybourn suggested the use of a few instruments, each one adapted to a particular type of surveying. He introduced double sights, which made it possible to backsight without turning the instrument on its staff, and he suggested the surveyor's cross for the use of laying out perpendicular lines and courses. The remaining surveyors of the century suggested rules and procedures which tended both to generalize the methods of survey and to give a higher degree of accuracy to their work. Eyre revealed the advantages in the greater use of logarithms and trigonometry in the calculations, and Love generalized the uses of the circumferentor and the method of surveying by taking the bearings of the sides of the enclosure.

Surveying instruments at the end of the seventeenth century were not essentially different from those in use at the beginning. During the early years some progress was made in reading small angles by means of concentric circles and diagonal lines drawn from a given point on the outer circle to a given point on the inner circle. Norden, Hopton, Rathborne, and Leybourn adapted the principle of the "topographicall instrument" to all the instruments of surveying: for example, the indices on the plane table and the new angle-measuring instrument known as the circumferentor. The instruments in use at the beginning of the century are clearly shown by Hopton, and those in use during the second half of the century are shown, with slight modifications, in cuts and diagrams by Rathborne.

For the measurement of length the standard was the line or cord until the chain of Rathborne, which was developed shortly before 1616, and which was followed by the chain of Edmund Gunter about 1620. Although both chains were used continuously, but not exclusively, throughout the remainder of the seventeenth century, Gunter's chain became firmly established by the close of the century and was preferred by a majority of the surveyors. The popularity of Gunter's chain is attested to by Sturmy: "Master Gunter's chain is a chain most used by surveyors of this age. . . ."[47] There is no doubt that the continued use of the chains of Rathborne, Gunter, Wing, and others using the statute rod contributed to the adoption of the statute rod of $16\frac{1}{2}$ feet in all forms of land measurements throughout England by the surveyors of the seventeenth and eighteenth centuries.

Along with the development of instruments for measuring angles and distances, a number of instruments were devised to aid the surveyor in plotting and in making his calculations. Among these were the sector, scales, and improved beam compasses. The scales were of various types divided into a given number of parts to the inch. A description and illustrations of these are usually included in the texts on surveying, as in Edmund Gunter's description of the sector and other scales.[48]

These instruments were frequently made by the mathematicians, and they were prized very highly by their owners, often being bequeathed to some friend at the death of the owner.[49]

[47] Samuel Sturmy, *Mathematical and Practical Arts* (London, 1669), Vol. 5, p. 3.
[48] Edmund Gunter, *The Works of Edmund Gunter*, 4th ed. (London, 1662), also Henry Coggeshall, *The Art of Practical Measuring* (London, 1722); and John Robertson, *A Treatise of Such Mathematical Instruments as are Usually Put into a Portable Case* (London, 1747).
[49] R. T. Gunther, *Early Science in Oxford, Part II, Mathematics* (Oxford, 1922), pp. 8–80. Gunther lists a large number of instrument makers of the seventeenth century with the dates of their most productive years.

The Eighteenth Century

General Background

By the beginning of the eighteenth century, education in England showed marked improvement over the early seventeenth century. A great part of the educational interest had shifted from the universities to the secondary schools, where the emphasis was placed on practical application of arithmetic, algebra, geometry, and trigonometry. Scientific knowledge barely existed among the upper classes of English society, and the pursuit of science did not constitute a profession in England. In most cases teachers were so poorly paid that they were compelled to exert their best efforts along some other line of endeavor in order to make a modest living. Important governmental scientific positions were filled by men who were amateurs, or who possessed only a small amount of scientific knowledge, or whose interest was primarily political rather than scientific. Charles Babbage asserted that there was no encouragement or demand from the English government for scientists, and that in order to obtain the best position one had to have a financial standing or play politics.[1]

[1] Charles Babbage, *Reflections on the Decline of Science in England* (London, 1830), pp. 37 ff.

By the close of the seventeenth century, however, the development of elementary mathematics had reached its modern stature. Arithmetic and numerical computations, with respect to commercial and practical work, had attained a point comparable to that of today. In the process of computation, decimal fractions were understood and were consistently used in numerical calculations. The old scratch method of division of numbers had been replaced by modern methods of division, and longer numerical calculations were done with ease by logarithms, which had been developed almost a century before. Elementary geometry had advanced to its present state of development, the reforms generally taking place in the secondary schools.[2]

In the second half of the eighteenth century the texts of William Leybourn played a great part in the education in geometry. One important aspect of the teaching of geometry in relation to surveying was the generalization of the rules and formulas for finding areas of plane figures and mensuration, and these methods were given in detail in the practical texts on geometry used by surveyors and artisans.[3] Trigonometry was well advanced both in theory and in practical application to surveying; adequate tables had been constructed so that the greatest use could be made of the subject.

Although great strides had been made in mathematics and its teaching, there was still little instruction given in surveying, and instruction in mathematics with particular reference to its use in surveying was frequently hard to obtain. As late as 1770, William Emerson in his text on surveying[4] gives a

[2] Florence Yeldham, *The Teaching of Arithmetic Through Four Hundred Years* (*1535–1935*) (London, 1936), pp. 1–143.

[3] F. W. Kokomoor, "The Distinctive Seventeenth Century Geometry," *Isis, 10* (1923), 367–415.

[4] William Emerson, *The Art of Surveying* (London, 1770), pp. 136–138.

143

course of study for prospective surveyors and sums up his comments by stating that thorough instruction should be had in arithmetic, geometry, and trigonometry before the study or practice of surveying is begun. At the same time, he deplores the condition of all sciences in England in comparison with their development in the Continental countries.

The development of surveying practice is determined to some extent on the amount of land surveying required, which in turn depends somewhat upon the condition and progress of agriculture. Although agriculture and the conditions of the English farmers had steadily advanced from the Norman Conquest to the last half of the seventeenth century, they were still in a deplorable state. Important among the factors retarding agricultural development were the disastrous Civil Wars, a lack of trained leadership in agricultural pursuits, a continued use of the open-field methods of cultivation over large areas of the best and most fertile lands in England, the small outlay of capital for agricultural purposes, and the almost nonexistent dissemination of agricultural knowledge.

During the last quarter of the seventeenth and the early part of the eighteenth centuries, English agriculture began to change. An increase in the population together with the changing eating habits of the English people necessitated greater production of food, which resulted in increased profits from agricultural pursuits. At the same time many farm laborers were leaving the farms and entering the manufacturing pursuits which were developing throughout the country. These and other factors brought about many changes in the landed gentry and in the distribution of the arable land among its owners. Much of the land which had been distributed among small owners was either sold or reverted back to the original owners. In the meantime, Parliament passed a number of enclosing acts which hastened the process of consolidating the small holding into larger estates which could be operated with greater efficiency. Although the process of enclosing was vigorously opposed, it reached its height and its near-completion in the eighteenth century.

With enclosure progressing, the demand for surveying increased. At the beginning of the eighteenth century, it was estimated that there were at least ten million acres of uncultivated land in England. The division of this uncultivated land and the attempted reclamation and drainage of the fen districts required a greater number of trained surveyors; there was a concomitant demand for improvement in techniques, methods, and accuracy of operations by the surveyors.[5]

One of the urgent problems confronting the instrument makers of the eighteenth century was a method of dividing linear and circular scales quickly and accurately. Solution of this problem would furnish the surveyor with an inexpensive instrument with a relatively high degree of accuracy.

Instrument Construction during the First Half of the Eighteenth Century

Although the method of triangulation from fixed bases reduced the number of linear measurements to a minimum, any error in the base line and vertical or horizontal angles would seriously affect the accuracy of the work as a whole.

[5] Roland E. Prothero, *English Farming Past and Present* (London, 1912), pp. 140–170; 207 ff.

The increased use of triangulation in surveying brought about an even greater demand for accuracy in angle measurements, and instrument makers and designers were called upon for the construction of instruments which would meet this requirement.

As far as can be determined, the need for increased accuracy and the attempts to correct this deficiency in angle measurements produced little change in construction and design until the close of the first quarter of the eighteenth century. H. D. Haskold, in a discussion of the development of mine-surveying instruments, states that there was no advance in the development of the theodolite from Leonard Digges, about 1555, to Jonathan Sisson (1694?–1749), about 1725.[6] The effect of poor instrument construction is voiced as late as 1727, in the fifth edition of Leybourn's *Compleat Surveyor*, edited by Samuel Cunn: "Lastly, I shall only add, that in a performance of this kind, Errors for the most part arise from the defects of Instruments: in the Framing, Dividing and Contriving.[7]

Some writers believe that Picard had substituted the telescope for plane sights as early as 1669 and that John Flamsteed had introduced spider web as lines in the focal plane of the telescope in 1689.[8] It is possible that Picard used the telescope in some instances for plane sights, but it is doubtful that it was widely applied to surveying instruments. Equally

[6] "Discussion of Mr. Dunbar Scott's Paper on Mine Surveying Instruments," *Transactions, Institution of Mining Engineers, 24* (1895), 504–523.

[7] Leybourn, *The Compleat Surveyor*, 5th ed., ed. by Samuel Cunn (London, 1727), Appendix, p. 142. Samuel Cunn, who flourished as a teacher of mathematics about 1720, is also known as a surveyor. He was the first master of Neale's Mathematical School for Boys in Fleet Street. Taylor, *Mathematical Practitioners*, pp. 305–306.

[8] Nicolas Bion, *Traité de la Construction et les Principaux Usages des Instrumentes de Mathématique* (Paris, 1709), translated by Edmund Stone (London, 1723), pp. 132–133.

unlikely is the use of spider web for cross hairs before the early part of the eighteenth century.[9] In any case, the first definite illustration of an improved theodolite combining the important inventions of the previous century is one of Jonathan Sisson's, probably constructed about 1720. Sisson, a well-known English instrument maker with shops in the Strand in London, did his principal work during the first half of the eighteenth century, and the first improved theodolite seems to have appeared during the 1720's. In Samuel Cunn's revised edition of Leybourn's *Compleat Surveyor*, Cunn states in the Appendix: "Therefore I think it proper to say, that I have seen a Theodolite made by Mr. Sisson, . . . for accuracy and Dispatch, fitter for a Surveyor than any other I have yet seen."[10]

Sisson developed and improved his theodolite by stages. Lawrence in his surveying text of 1721 gives a line drawing of an instrument, probably about 1720, by Sisson.[11] This theodolite was of the cradle type. Gardiner's *Surveying* describes an improved theodolite which was developed before 1732.[12] A line drawing of a theodolite by Sisson is given in the text facing the title page and seems to follow the description in the text. An even more advanced instrument is in the collection of the Science Museum, London (Fig. 30). Its illustration indicates some of the improvements over the line drawings of Lawrence and Gardiner. These

[9] Bion, *op. cit.*, pp. 126–127.

[10] Leybourn, ref. 7, Appendix, Book X, p. 143. Jonathan Sisson (1694?–1749) specialized in the designing and construction of optical and mathematical instruments of a high degree of perfection in his shops in the Strand. He was an expert at the precise dividing of scales. Several of his instruments are in the Science Museum in London. Taylor, *Mathematical Practitioners*, p. 306.

[11] Edward Lawrence, *The Young Surveyors Guide: or a New Introduction to the Whole Art of Land Surveying* (London, 1721).

[12] William Gardiner, *Practical Surveying Improved: or Land Measuring According to the Most Correct Methods* (London, 1732).

Fig. 30. A mid-eighteenth-century theodolite constructed by
Jonathan Sisson. Photograph of the original in the
Science Museum, South Kensington, London.
(Courtesy of the Director. Crown copyright reserved.)

improvements are (*a*) a shorter telescope, (*b*) the addition
of a bubble level on the telescope, (*c*) the addition of a
pinion to set the vernier on the horizontal limb, and (*d*) a
general compactness of the body of the instrument which
would give greater stability and less shake to the theodolite
in its operation.

Little is known of Sisson's method of construction but it is certain that his instruments were hand divided. His theodolites and levels were considered standard until the time of Jesse Ramsden, and Sisson was one of the most respected craftsmen of the first half of the eighteenth century.

While Sisson was improving the theodolite and using the telescope in its construction, Chester Moor Hall,[13] discovered the achromatic lens and its application to the telescope. An unsigned article in the *Gentleman's Magazine*[14] states that Hall arrived at his invention by considering the human eye and the fluids surrounding it and thereby constructing an object glass similar to the eye. This writer asserts that Hall was able to construct several object glasses with an aperture of $2\frac{1}{2}$ inches and a focal length of 20 inches. Jonathan Sisson may have used one of Hall's acromatic lenses on his improved theodolite.[15]

Great strides were made in the construction of surveying instruments during the first half of the eighteenth century, but the new surveying texts of the same period reveal that

[13] Chester Moor Hall (1703-1771) is described on his tombstone as a "judicious lawyer, able mathematician, a polite scholar and magistrate of strictest sincerity." *DNB.*

[14] Unsigned article, "Chester Moor Hall," *Gentleman's Magazine and Historical Chronicle, 50* (1790), Part II, 890-891.

[15] Although Hall is usually given credit for the achromatic lens, the subject had been investigated for many years previous to Hall by Sir Isaac Newton (1642-1727) and Leonhard Euler (1707-1783) but their experiments proved fruitless. Further work was done by the Swede, S. Klingenstierna, and published about 1754. Klingenstierna showed the errors in the experiments of Newton and Euler and suggested that with glass and water there could be color without refraction. It is doubtful that Hall had seen the results of these experiments before he completed his investigations. Article on lenses in *Edinburgh Encyclopaedia* conducted by David Brewster (Edinburgh, 1830), p. 140; and S. Klingenstierna, "Anmerkung über das Gesetz der Brechung der Lichtstrahlen von Verschiedener Art, *Der Königlich-Schwedischen Akademie der Wissenchaften Abhandlungen, 10* (1753), 300-309.

149

the surveyors had not kept up with the instrument makers. Although the surveyors were insisting on greater accuracy in their instruments, they constantly reverted back to surveying by the chain only.

Surveying Texts of the First Half of the Eighteenth Century

Of the several works on surveying published in the first half of the eighteenth century, four were reprints of seventeenth-century works and one was an important related work. The reprints were of the works of John Norden, John Love, Adam Martindale, and the fifth edition of Leybourn's *Compleat Surveyor*, edited by Samuel Cunn. The first three differed little from their first editions, but that of Leybourn shows a complete rearrangement of the original work and the addition of an appendix. Although a work first published in 1725 with the title, *The Practical Surveyor*, names John Hammond as its author, the preface of the fourth edition of that book states that the major portion of all the editions was composed by Samuel Cunn, who "for some reason let it appear under the name of John Hammond who was a clerk to his friend Mr. Charles Brent."[16] The discussion of surveying in this text differs but little from that of Cunn's edition of Leybourn's *Compleat Surveyor*.

The first original text on surveying published in the eighteenth century was Edward Lawrence's *The Young Surveyors' Guide*, published in 1716 and reprinted in 1717. This text discusses surveying in a manner similar to Leybourn's and the better texts of the late seventeenth century.

---

[16] John Hammond, *The Practical Surveyor* (London, 1731).

Lawrence published another work (1731) devoted primarily to the business of stewards and overseers of large estates and manors. Only 18 of the 319 pages of this text are devoted to the actual survey.[17]

Both of Lawrence's texts emphasize the importance of observing errors in the survey; the greatest errors occur from surveying with the plane table. If all the angles and stationary lines are carefully measured and if the sum of the stationary lines does not exceed four miles, then an error of at least one chain can be detected. Lawrence does not state how this error will be detected—possibly by protraction and the lack of closure—but he mentions that many surveys will show errors as high as 1 in 40 and sometimes as high as 1 in 20. Errors frequently arise from a lack of horizontal leveling of the instruments; to remedy this Lawrence strongly advises the use of Sisson's improved theodolite.

One of the most important related texts written in the first half of the eighteenth century was a small pamphlet by Thomas Burgh,[18] which contains a method of determining the area of an irregular right-lined figure without breaking the figure up into a large number of simple figures.

First defining the terms northings, southings, eastings, and westings, Burgh gives a method of determining the extreme North, South, East, and West points. He then goes through a discussion of the areas of irregular figures and proceeds to give a proof of the double meridian method of determining the area of a right-lined figure, which is virtually the same as that used at the present time. His method for finding areas is summed up as follows:[19]

[17] Edward Lawrence, *The Duty and Office of a Land Stewart* (London, 1731).

[18] Thomas Burgh, *A Method to Determine the Area of Right-lined Figures Universally* (London, 1724).

[19] Burgh, *op. cit.,* p. 7.

CHAPTER SIX

To find the Area of any Right-lined Figure

1. Let every particular Easting between any two adjacent Stations be drawn into the Semi-Sun of the absolute Northing of the same two Stations, and collect the Sum of such Rectangles.
2. Let every particular Westing between two adjacent Stations be drawn into the Semi-Sum of the absolute Northing of the Stations, and collect the Sum of such Rectangles.
3. The difference of the two Sums is equal to the Area sought.

It is noteworthy that this method of determining the area does not appear in any surveying text until the second half of the eighteenth century, and then only as an alternative method. The text carries twelve pages of latitudes and departures for angles for every one-quarter degree. There was no point in giving the tables to a smaller unit, stated Burgh, for the instruments could not measure to a higher degree of accuracy.

Following the publication of Burgh's pamphlet, two texts were published, similar in nature, which stressed surveying by the chain only instead of by angle-measuring instruments. The first of these texts, by Henry Wilson, was published in 1732,[20] and the second, by John Gray, was published in 1737.[21]

While placing the greatest emphasis on surveying by the chain, Wilson also discusses the survey by angle-measuring instruments. In this discussion Wilson gives Burgh's double area rule for computing areas as an alternative method of computing the areas of irregular figures. This is probably the first time the double area method of computing areas had appeared in an English surveying text.

[20] Henry Wilson, *Geodaesia Catenea: or Surveying by the Chain Only* (London, 1732).
[21] John Gray, *The Art of Land-Measuring Explained* (Glasgow, 1737).

Gray's *Art of Land-Measuring* follows the same general trend as Wilson's *Surveying by the Chain*. However, Gray is a greater advocate of surveying by the chain than Wilson, arguing that the radii of the angle-measuring instruments are so small that accurate results cannot be obtained. He goes into great detail in discussing these errors and asserts that an angle can be determined to an accuracy of 6′ of arc with the chain, whereas the best that can be expected from the theodolite is 10′. It appears that the author was not familiar with the improved theodolite of Sisson, which was reputed to give readings of angle to 6′ of arc.

Gray's work is important in that it gives clear-cut methods of conducting the survey. Errors arising in the survey are discussed, and simple checks are suggested for their correction. He states that with care in the use of the chain, accuracy to 1 in 1,000 can be obtained whereas an accuracy of 1 in 900 is permissible.

In contrast to the works of Wilson and Gray, the last two texts on surveying in the first half of the sixteenth century discuss in detail surveying with angle-measuring instruments. The first of these, *The Practical Surveyor*, by William Gardiner,[22] a self-styled surveyor, was published in 1737.

An important feature of Gardiner's text is a clear and detailed description of Sisson's improved theodolite and level with instructions for their uses. This discussion is followed by the methods of surveying large tracts of land, and Gardiner asserts that the theodolite should be used in these surveys. In the survey of small enclosures or single fields Gardiner prefers to use the circumferentor, plane table, or chain only. In addition to the description of Sisson's theodolite, Gardiner's text is significant in that the author stresses the need for careful work in the survey and assures the

[22] William Gardiner, *Practical Surveying Improved: or Land Measuring According to the Most Correct Methods* (London, 1737).

reader that a survey of 10 miles with 200 stations can be made to close within one-half chain. Finally, Gardiner is the first English author to argue against using the superficial or surface area of hills and valleys of the enclosure, but he insists that since all kinds of vegetation tends to grow perpendicularly to the horizontal rather than to the surface of hillsides and valleys that the plane or plan area should be used.

In 1739 Robert Gibson published *A Treatise on Land Surveying*[23] which was the sixth and last work on surveying in the first half of the eighteenth century. This work was the first English surveying text also to be published in the North American colonies. The American edition was published in Philadelphia in 1785 as the fourth edition and was sold by Joseph Cruikshank.[24]

In his fourth edition Gibson prefers one of the angle-measuring instruments for measuring angles, proceeding around the land, keeping the enclosure always to the right of the operator. He illustrates the advantages of Burgh's method of computing the area by the double-area method—a method which makes the use of an angle-measuring instrument necessary. At this point, Gibson discusses the checks on closure—the sum of the Northings must equal the sum of the Southings and the sum of the Eastings equal the sum of the Westings—and offers a general rule for correction. He gives a general check for the accuracy of the work in small surveys and states that if the sum as stated above is greater than one-fifth of a perch for each station, the survey must be made anew. If the error is less than this,

[23] Robert Gibson, *A Treatise on Land Surveying* (Dublin, 1739).
[24] Robert Gibson, *A Treatise of Practical Surveying* (Philadelphia, 1785). This, the fourth English edition, was followed by 21 American editions and reprints up to 1839. L. C. Karpinski, *Bibliography of Mathematical Works Printed in America Through 1850* (Ann Arbor, 1940), pp. 82–85.

he gives a rule for correction as follows: find the latitude and departure for each course, "observing to add on half the difference to the numbers in the lower columns, and to subtract it from those of the greater, in such manner as that each station may be altered nearly in proportion to its length." There is no attempt to correct the angles of the survey.

Gibson's work brings to a close the first half of the eighteenth century. Although several important texts were published during this period, there was a tendency to revert to surveying by the chain only rather than with angle-measuring instruments. These texts did stress the importance of accuracy in the survey and the partial acceptance of Burgh's method of computing the areas of irregular figures.

Instrument construction advanced with the development of the improved theodolite of Sisson, which carried the expertly hand-divided circular scales. The telescope now was a permanent fixture of the theodolite and increased the precision of its operation. These developments accelerated the continued advances in surveying instruments through the next half of the century.

Second Half of the Eighteenth Century

With the increase in population during the first half of the eighteenth century, an acceleration of enclosing, the removal of many barriers to the legal transfer of property, and the great industrial advancements made throughout the nation, there was an ever-increasing demand for food and agricultural products of all kinds. This demand naturally resulted in greater agricultural activity, which tended to increase the value of the lands.[25] Consequently, there was a

[25] Ernest L. Bogart, *Economic History of Europe 1760–1939* (New York, 1942), pp. 1–150.

pressing need for greater accuracy in surveying. To a certain extent, this need is clearly reflected in the texts on surveying written during the second half of the century. During this time, five new texts, eleven reprints of texts from the first half of the century, and two reprints or editions of a sixteenth-century text were published.

The original texts advocate a procedure which had become popular in the first half of the century, namely, the practice of surveying by the chain only, or, as it was frequently called at the time, of *surveying by the long-lines*. These texts, however, illustrate certain tendencies in surveying by their emphasis on the importance of accurate measurements, surveying with offsets, and adapting Burgh's rule for computing areas by double areas. Four of the five texts published during the last half of the eighteenth century are similar to one another in most respects and will be discussed together, while the fifth by Arthur Burns will be considered separately.

Minor Publications

The surveying methods discussed in the four minor publications are principally surveying by chain; slight reference is to angle-measuring instruments. The first of this group, *An Essay on Practical Surveying*, by Benjamin Noble,[26] makes some important suggestions on the office work of the survey: (1) an improvement in protraction by dividing the plotting paper into a series of parallel and perpendicular lines; (2) a greater use of trigonometry in calculating the parts and areas of figures; and (3) when angle-measuring instruments have been used in the survey, the use of Burgh's method for calculating areas.

[26] Benjamin Noble, *Geodaesia Hibernica, or an Essay on Practical Surveying* (Dublin, 1763).

William Emerson's *The Art of Surveying*[27] is nothing more than a compendium of older texts with an appendix containing additions and corrections. Important among these additions are a suggested course of study in mathematics and surveying for young surveyors (see page 144), a method of triangulation for large estates using several stations and stationary lines which are to be measured with the chain or waywiser, and the computation of the plan areas of hills and valleys rather than their superficial areas.

Of these four writers, Benjamin Talbot in his *Art of Land-Measuring*[28] is the only surveyor to advocate the use of instruments which are entirely different from those used by other surveyors of the eighteenth century. Talbot states that he gave up surveying with the plane table, circumferentor, and theodolite and used instead the chain and a modified form of Hadley's sextant to measure angles. Later he modified the ordinary sextant into a form which was called the catoptric sextant and used this for measuring all angles in the survey. It is noteworthy that although Talbot used trigonometric methods in calculating the areas and parts of figures, he does not mention Burgh's method of determining the areas of irregular figures.

William Davis, the fourth of these minor writers, is a strong advocate of surveying by the chain only.[29] His text, published in 1798, does not mention angle-measuring instruments nor their use in surveying. The discussion of chain surveying, instructions to the surveyors, protracting the results of the survey, and the computation of areas follow closely the rules set down by Noble, Emerson, and Talbot.

[27] William Emerson, *The Art of Surveying or Measuring Land* (London, 1770).

[28] Benjamin Talbot, *The Compleat Art of Land-Measuring: or a Guide to Practical Surveying* (London, 1780).

[29] William Davis, *A Complete Treatise on Land Surveying by the Chain, Cross and Offset Staffs Only* (London, 1798).

Arthur Burns

A New and Correct Method of Surveying by Arthur Burns,[30] published in 1776, is probably the outstanding surveying text of the late eighteenth century. Its author was a strong exponent of survey by the chain only, although Part Two of his text gives a method for surveying with angle-measuring instruments.

In his "Introduction" Burns sums up his criticisms of surveying with angle-measuring instruments and gives his reasons for advocating surveying by the chain. He argues that the chain is the only instrument by which angles can be accurately measured; that the practice of surveying by the chain is easy to learn and use; that it is the quickest and cheapest method of surveying; that it does not require expensive instruments to perform the survey; that only the four fundamental operations of arithmetic are required to perform the calculations after a survey has been made with the chain; and, finally, that the operator does not have to pursue an extensive course in mathematics in order to become a surveyor.

Burns is probably at his best in discussing methods for finding the areas of, and plotting the results of, the survey, striving to obtain the greatest accuracy regardless of the methods used. In chain surveying, where the irregular figures have been broken down into triangles, geometric methods are employed for the computation of areas. If the survey has been conducted with an angle-measuring instrument such as the theodolite, where the bearings of the sides have been taken, Burgh's method is used to compute the area.

[30] Arthur Burns, *Geodaesia Improved: or, a New and Correct Method of Surveying Made Exceedingly Easy* (Chester, 1776).

It is noteworthy that whereas Burns ascribes all the errors of closure to angle-measuring instruments, correction of these errors is given for the lengths of the sides only. There is, however, no recognition of errors in the length of the chain or in the methods of measuring lengths. Burns' rules for the correction of the errors of closure are similar to those of Gibson.

Burns' work is important not in the methods of survey used, but in the following points: the setting down of certain principles of survey with regard to the rights of the land-owner and the tenants; the emphasis on conducting the survey, whether by the chain or with angle-measuring instruments, with the greatest possible accuracy in the determination of areas and the highest precision in plotting the map of the enclosure; and, finally, the stress on the advantages of Burgh's method of computing the area when an angle-measuring instrument has been used. In discussing the legal aspects of surveying, Burns follows custom rather than some specific law or laws regulating the action of surveyors.

Summary of Eighteenth-Century Surveying Methods

An examination of eighteenth-century surveying works reveals a definite tendency to use the earlier methods of surveying by the chain rather than the more highly precise angle-measuring instruments that had been developed and refined during the century. These earlier methods are clearly championed by Gray, Noble, Emerson, and Davis. Lawrence, Gardiner, Gibson, and others advocate the use of angle-measuring instruments, but such use was certainly best defined during the first half of the century.

Some of the factors bringing about the increased use of chain surveying can be traced to the changes in economic conditions. Although the enclosure movement had begun in the latter part of the fourteenth century, its maximum effects were not felt until the eighteenth century. This movement required a greater number of land surveyors out of the small supply which was then available, and the private teachers of surveying and the inadequate school system of the early eighteenth century were unable to turn out sufficient operators to meet the needs of the profession. Because of the increased demand for their services, surveyors sought to perform the work as quickly as possible, and chain surveying was considered to be much more rapid than instrument surveying.

Not only had angle-measuring instruments been developed to the point where they required a much greater technical skill for correct operation, but a thorough knowledge of the fundamental principles of geometry and trigonometry was required in order to perform the office work from the data obtained in a survey with these instruments. The development of instruments of precision rapidly increased their cost, making it difficult for many surveyors to equip themselves with all the instruments required for surveys. George Adams pointed out that the cost of the instruments needed by the average land surveyor at the close of the eighteenth century was over £125.[31] Finally, the agricultural class did not appreciate expensive, high-precision work in land surveying, resulting in reluctance on the part of the landowners to pay a professional fee for the accurate surveying of their lands.

The sixteenth century had produced the great instrument designer Leonard Digges and the renowned instrument maker Humphrey Cole, but it was left for several eminent Englishmen during the second half of the eighteenth century

[31] George Adams, *Geometrical and Graphical Essays* (London, 1797), pp. 182–190.

to complete the work initiated by these two. Two of these men, George Graham and John Bird, were probably the greatest exponents of hand dividing of instrument scales.

George Graham

A contemporary of Jonathan Sisson and a notable instrument maker, George Graham (1673–1751) did much to advance the construction of precision surveying instruments during the mid-eighteenth century.[32] After serving his apprenticeship, Graham attracted the attention of Thomas Tompson (1639–1713), a clockmaker, and on Tompson's death, Graham took over the business. Although generally known as a clockmaker, Graham devised and constructed a number of astronomical instruments as well as high-precision sidereal and mean time clocks. In 1725 he constructed for the Royal Observatory an 8-foot quadrant which was made of iron and could be read, by means of a vernier, to about 15′ of arc. He also made small instruments and levels.

Graham's method of scale division was continued bisection regardless of whether the scale was straight line or circular. This method is important, since it is the first method of hand dividing of which any exact and definite information is known. For the division of a circular arc, the method is as follows:

Two concentric arcs of radii 96.85″ and 95.8″ respectively were first described by the beam compass. On the inner of these arcs, 90° was to be divided into degrees and twelfth parts of a degree while the same on the outer was to be divided into 96 equal parts, and these again into sixteenth parts. The reason for adopting the latter was that 96 and 16 both being powers of 2, the

[32] C. Doris Hellman, "George Graham Maker of Horological and Astronomical Instruments," *Vassar Journal of Undergraduate Studies*, 5 (1931), 221–251; Taylor, *Mathematical Practitioners*, pp. 289–290.

divisions will be got at by continual bisection alone, which, in Graham's opinion, who first employed it, is the only accurate method, and would thus serve as a check upon the accuracy of the divisions of the outer arc. With the same distance on the beam compass as was used to describe the inner arc, laid off from 0°, the point 60° was at once determined.

With the points 0° and 60° as centers successively, and a distance on the beam compass very nearly bisecting the arc of 60°, two slight marks were made on the arc; the distance between these marks was carefully divided by hand, aided by a lens, and this gives the point 30°. The chord of 60° laid off from the point 30° gave the point 90°, and the quadrant was now divided into three resulting divisions again trisected, giving 18 parts of 5° each. Each of the quinquesected gave degrees, the twelfth part of which were arrived at by bisecting and trisecting as before. The outer arc was divided by continual bisection alone, and a table was constructed by which the readings of the one arc could be converted into those of the other. After the dots indicating the required divisions were obtained, either straight strokes, all directed towards the center, were drawn through them by the dividing knife, or sometimes small arcs were drawn through them by the beam compass having its fixed point somewhere on the line which was a tangent to the quadrantal arc at the point where a division was to be marked.[33]

The most important instrument used by Graham in this work was a beam compass, considered by its maker to be trustworthy to 0.00062 of an inch when used with a microscope. In these instruments the jaws were moved by means of a micrometer, and a microscope was used with it. Here for the first time the dividing of the circle had become sufficiently important in relation to other instrument details to attract the attention of capable and patient technicians who finally were able to reach a high degree of perfection in hand dividing.

[33] R. Smith, *Compleat System of Optics* (London, 1738), Vol. 2, pp. 332–336.

John Bird

The third master technician of this period was John Bird,[34] who probably carried hand dividing to its peak of perfection. Bird worked for Jonathan Sisson and was instructed and encouraged in his work by George Graham; he probably took over Graham's work at his death. Bird's method of dividing was somewhat different from Graham's but is similar to it in the use of bisections. Bird's general method is illustrated in his 8-foot quadrant, constructed about 1767, where he constructed his divided arc by means of protracted radii and computed chords.[35]

Although hand dividing reached its peak of perfection under Bird, there was criticism of his method. John Smeaton (1724–1792), the eminent engineer, criticized the method for its lack of unity of principle: Bird had proceeded partly on the principle of a protracted radius and partly on that of a computed chord; the two principles, Smeaton pointed out, may not agree.[36] A modification of Bird's method, obviating the criticisms of Smeaton, was utilized in the construction of instruments by John Troughton (*ca.* 1747–*ca.* 1790).[37] Although Bird's genius was primarily directed to the building of astronomical instruments and to the estab-

[34] Bird (1709–1776), the eminent English instrument maker, constructed some of the instruments used by Mason and Dixon in surveying the boundary between Maryland and Pennsylvania. C. Doris Hellman, "John Bird, Mathematical Instrument Maker in the Strand," *Isis*, 17 (1932), 127–152; *DNB*.

[35] For a detailed discussion of Birds' method of dividing, see W. Ludlum, "An Introduction and Notes on Mr. Bird's Method of Dividing, *Philosophical Transactions*, 99 (1800), Part I, 105–143.

[36] John Smeaton, "Observations on the Graduations of Astronomical Instruments," *Royal Society of London. Philosophical Transactions*, 76 (1786), 1–47.

[37] Edward Troughton, "An Account of the Method of Dividing Astronomical and Other Instruments," *Philosophical Transactions*, 109 (1809), 105–143.

lishment of the standard of length, he probably contributed as well to the construction of surveying instruments. In 1767 Bird published, by order of the Commissioners of Longitude, *The Method of Dividing Astronomical Instruments*.[38] This pamphlet was written primarily for practical workmen.

H. D. Haskold credits Bird with developing a slow motion or tangent screw which was attached to Sisson's large mural arc.[39] This attachment made it possible to observe an additional number of seconds which were not indicated by the vernier but which could be determined by means of the turns of the screwhead. Haskold also states that the same plan was used by Bird in the construction of his mural quadrant. It is possible that Bird was the first to use this means of determining the precise reading of an angle; however, R. T. Gunther states that in 1649 Francis Potter of Trinity College, Oxford, made a compass with a head and a screw that, with slow motion, would move the points of the compasses very slowly. In fact, it made it possible to divide an inch into one thousand parts.[40]

The Achromatic Lens

While these improvements were being made in the dividing of circular arcs, John and Peter Dollond[41] rediscovered the achromatic lens, invented by Chester Moor Hall, and applied it to the telescope. By using two kinds of glass in the construction of lenses, the Dollonds made it possible to overcome both spherical aberration and the errors arising

[38] Ludlum, ref. 35.

[39] H. D. Haskold, "Remarks upon Surveying Instruments," *Transactions American Institute of Mining Engineers, 31* (1902), 76 ff.

[40] R. T. Gunther, *Early Science in Oxford, Part II, Mathematics* (Oxford, 1922), pp. 30–32.

[41] John Dollond (1706–1761) was a self-educated man in languages, mathematics, optics, and astronomy. For the reinvention of the achromatic lens, he was awarded the Copley Medal, and in 1761 he became a member of the Royal Society. *DNB*.

from varying refrangibility. Regardless of whether Roger Bacon in 1290, Porta in 1561, Digges in 1570, the Dutch in 1608, or Galileo in 1609 invented the telescope, the important fact is that Hall in 1733 and Dollond again in 1758 invented the achromatic lens and made the telescope practical for use as an attachment to angle-measuring instruments. With the addition of cross hairs or wires, the telescope became an exact instrument for precise measurements of angular distances.

The Stadia

In the development of the telescope, Gascoigne used two movable straight edges in his micrometer. It is possible that Hooke suggested using human hair and that David Rittenhouse was the first to suggest spider web for cross hairs, but it seems certain that William Green, a London optician, put to use Geminiano Montanari's earlier discovery of placing several equidistant threads upon the diaphragm of the telescope. It is doubtful that Green knew of the previous discovery of Montanari, but it is certain that this principle was rediscovered by Green and published in 1778.[42] Here Green explains that, with a given number of threads or intervals in the focus of the telescope, a given distance on a rod could be read, this ascertaining the distance of the rod from the instrument.

The first practical application of the principle of the stadia was by James Watt in the Tarbert Crinan lines, 1771. In a published account Watt gives a description of the instrument that he used in this work.[43] The telescope had

[42] William Green, *Description and Use of an Improved Refracting Telescope with Scale for Surveying* (London, 1778).

[43] James Patrick Muirhead, *The Origin and Progress of the Mechanical Inventions of James Watt* (London, 1854), Vol. 1, pp. 131–146; H. D. Haskold, "Remarks Upon Surveying Instruments," *Transactions American Institute of Mining Engineers, 31* (1902), 76 ff.

an object glass of 12 inches, an eyeglass of 1½ inches focus, and a magnification of eight times. In the focus of the eyeglass there were two parallel horizontal hairs, placed about ⅒ inch apart and perpendicular to a vertical hair. With this arrangement of the telescope, Watt constructed a 12-foot rod and calibrated it to read the horizontal distance of the rod from the instrument in feet or chains. The construction of the instrument and the calibrations on the rod gave an accuracy of one one-hundredth of the total distance. Watt preferred this method of measuring distance because it gave all distances with equal accuracy; it gave better accuracy on uneven ground; it was much better for hilly or mountainous country; and it was much more satisfactory where there were water inlets.

Dividing by Instrument during the Late Eighteenth Century

Addition of the achromatic lens and a method of measuring the subtended distance by means of the stadia, parallel hairs, or wires made the telescope an instrument that could be used for exacting angular measurements. It now remained for the instrument technicians to develop some means of dividing the circle mechanically so that most of the errors encountered in hand dividing might be eliminated and the time required for the construction of the instruments lessened to the point where small instruments could be constructed accurately and in quantity.

In the mid-eighteenth century, all graduations were made by hand. They consisted of two types: original graduation and copying. The original graduations were performed by the hand method given above and practiced by nearly all hand dividers—a method reaching perfection under Sisson, Graham, and Bird. In copying, a carefully divided circle was used for the copy, and the circular plate on which the copy was to be made was attached to this plate. An index was fixed to the center of these two plates, and, as it passed around, the divisions were cut on the smooth plate with a knife. This method in itself produced many errors, even when the original plate had been accurately divided. On the other hand, the method of original graduations for highly accurate results was an extremely slow and tedious process. Bird's method of constructing a 4-foot quadrant took approximately 52 days of hard and patient labor to divide the circular arc. If a stepping or roller method was used to locate the original divisions and a process of checking was used afterwards, it would require about 150 days to check all the points on the quadrant.

In order to overcome this time- and labor-consuming process, a number of attempts were made to develop a mechanical method of dividing circular arcs. We are probably indebted to the clockmakers for the general idea of a cutting machine. In most cases, their problem was not so much one of accuracy in cutting out the notches in their wheels as it was one of finding a method that would perform the job in a minimum of time. In the *Cyclopaedia of Useful Arts* there is a description of an early type of a machine used for this purpose.[44]

According to M. Julien Leroy in *Étrennes Chronométriques*,[45] Robert Hooke in 1675 was the first to contrive an apparatus which could be really called a cutting machine. This machine was constructed in the principle of the endless screw, but it failed because Hooke was never able to obtain

[44] "Culling Engines," *The Cyclopaedia, or Universal Dictionary of the Arts, Sciences, and Literature*, Adam Rees, ed. (London, 1819).

[45] Antoine Thiout, *Traité d'Horlogerie* (Paris, 1741), Vol. 2, pp. 327–400 and Julien Leroy, *Règle Artificielle du Temps, Traité* (New edition, Paris, 1737), pp. 370–433.

accurate work in the mechanical details of the apparatus. It should be noted, however, that Hooke's principles were used in constructing later dividing machines. There are references in French literature during the early part of the eighteenth century to various improvements made in machines for cutting the teeth in clocks, and Smeaton mentions that in 1741 Henry Hindley of York had constructed a cutting engine.[46] This machine indented the edge of a circle in such manner that a screw with fifteen threads acting at once could be used to read off any number of divisions on the circle. Somewhat later a Frenchman, the Duc de Chaulnes, developed a method of dividing the circle which was a remarkable improvement and is the foundation of our present method of examining and computing the errors in our divided circles.[47] This method, published in 1768, involves replacing the points of the beam compasses by two micrometer microscopes which had cross wires or hairs in the focus of the eyepiece of the microscope. These microscopes were fixed fast to a frame and were set to read diametrically opposite points on the circle to be divided. Two strips of brass, each carrying a finely engraved line, were fixed temporarily to the circle edge. The divisions on the brass were bisected as nearly as possible by the cross hairs in the microscope, and divisions were made at these bisections. The circle was then rotated through 180°, and the necessary adjustments were made in the microscopes and brass strips until the opposite divisions were again bisected by the hairs in the microscope. If a cutting frame were fixed to the stand carrying the circle to be divided, it would only be necessary to cut the divisions opposite

[46] John Smeaton, ref. 36. Robert S. Woodbury, *History of the Gear-Cutting Machine* (Cambridge, 1958), pp. 45–59.

[47] M. le Duc de Chaulnes, *Nouvelle méthode pour diviser les instruments de mathématiques et d'astronomie* (Paris, 1768), pp. 411–454.

the bisected divisions on the brass strips with the aid of the microscopes to obtain two diametrically opposite points. By bisections and trisections, all done by careful trial and adjustment, it was possible to fill in the subdivisions in a most precise manner. Once an accurate division of one circle was obtained, this circle could be used as a master circle to make other divided circles by the same method.

Jesse Ramsden

The works of Hooke, the Duc de Chaulnes, and Hindley no doubt had a great influence on the instrument maker Jesse Ramsden,[48] who developed the first successful dividing machine or engine. Ramsden probably opened his instrument shop in London about 1760. His work was notably accurate and gave excellent results, but his methods were slow, tedious, difficult, and required exceptional skill and patience. Ramsden's method was to divide his circles, by means of beam compasses, as accurately as possible; then, by means of microscopes, he ascertained the errors which were corrected, where possible, by pressing over the original dots, either backwards or forwards, with a steel point in his hand. This method is called "coaxing."

Demand for Ramsden's instruments became so great that he began to devise a mechanical means of dividing the circle. Ramsden doubtless was familiar with the work of Hooke, the Duc de Chaulnes, Hindley, and others in constructing dividing engines, and no doubt the reward given by the Board of Longitude to Bird for his dividing method must have been an added incentive. Since the general principle

[48] Jesse Ramsden (1735–1800) was apprenticed first as a cloth-maker but in 1758 he apprenticed himself in London as an instrument maker. Ramsden took out many patents on the improvement of instruments and was renowned throughout the world as an instrument maker. *DNB*.

of the dividing engine had been developed, it was Ramsden's task to utilize these ideas and to perfect the mechanical apparatus in such a manner that the machine would be practical, performing the dividing quickly and with a high degree of precision. The first engine was completed by 1768 but after a number of tests, its accuracy was questionable. In 1775 Ramsden constructed a second engine, with minor changes, which met his requirements. The first engine, similar to the one shown in Fig. 31, had a notched horizontal plate 30 inches in diameter and was probably used by Ramsden for theodolites and instruments which did not require an exceedingly high degree of accuracy.[49]

In constructing the dividing engine, Ramsden's first problem was the construction of a machine to cut the teeth in the circumference of the horizontal plate of the dividing engine and to cut the screw which operated this plate. This machine, one of the earliest applications of the principle for changing the lateral speed of a tool in cutting a screw by differential wheels, is described in a pamphlet by Ramsden.[50]

The dividing engine which was finally developed (Fig. 31) consists of a horizontal bronze plate, 45 inches in diameter, which rotates on a vertical axis and has an outer edge ratcheted or cut into 2,160 (6 × 360) teeth into which an endless screw gears. This screw, which turns the plate, is operated by a treadle whose downward stroke can be adjusted by a mechanism for turning the screw through any part of a revolution. A free wheel on the screw axis allows the screw to remain stationary on the upward move-

[49] This improved dividing engine with the screw-cutting gear is now preserved in the Smithsonian Institution. J. Elfreth Watkins, "The Ramsden Dividing Engine," *Annual Report of the Smithsonian Institution* (Washington, 1891), p. 732.

[50] Jesse Ramsden, *Description of an Engine for the Division of Mathematical Instruments*, published by order of the Commissioners of Longitude (London, 1777), p. 14.

Fig. 31. Jesse Ramsden's dividing machine constructed about
1775. Photograph from the original at the Smithsonian
Institution.
(Courtesy of the Smithsonian Institution.)

ment of the treadle. The work to be divided was firmly fixed to the plate and was made concentric with it. The divisions were cut, while the screw was stationary, by a cutting point carried in a frame which allows only a radial to-and-fro motion of the cutting point. In this manner the operator could divide very rapidly by alternately depressing the treadle and working the dividing knife.

Ramsden divided a sextant with the dividing engine so successfully that the Commissioners of Longitude offered him a reward on the condition that the engine be at the service of the instrument makers and that Ramsden publish an explanation of his method of constructing the dividing engine as well as his method of dividing circles. The pamphlet was published in 1777, and Ramsden was paid £615 as the reward. He also devised a machine for dividing linear scales, which embodied with slight changes the same principles used in the first engine. In 1793 Edward Troughton constructed a dividing engine with a smaller plate than Ramsden's but with many of the details simplified. Several other dividing engines were constructed in England and on the Continent following that of Ramsden and embodying his fundamental principles.

The dividing engine was only one of Ramsden's contributions to surveying instruments. He constructed one of the most satisfactory geodetic theodolites, to be described later, developed before the close of the eighteenth century; he made it possible to light the wires of the transit; he developed means of correcting the errors of collimation of the theodolite; he developed an improved type of pyrometer; and he was the first to apply reading off microscopes to circular instruments. It may have been Chester Moor Hall and John Dollond who sent pure light streaming through the soul of the telescope, but it was Ramsden who graduated its sensitive brain.

Topographical Surveys
during the Eighteenth Century

Throughout the eighteenth century, and particularly in the second half of the century, land surveying had reached a relatively high degree of accuracy and ease in operation. However, the techniques of the surveyors for regional maps and topographical surveys were little better, if as good, as those of the land surveyors. For the measurement of distances, the topographical surveyors generally preferred the holometer or wheel perambulator, with which the distances would be determined by the recorded number of revolutions of a wheel multiplied by its circumference. As might be expected, these methods gave highly unsatisfactory results. Many of the regional maps were constructed by means of such road traverses with cross bearings to a number of stations with the plane table, circumferentor, or the magnetic compass with peephole sights for aligning the instrument on a distant object. In some cases the distances were still determined by viewing; that is, the operator would go to an elevated spot and estimate the distance by sighting with the naked eye. This situation was due in part to a lack of cooperation of the central government for topographical surveys. Not until later did the government recognize the need for these surveys, and then the Ordnance Survey was established.[51]

Although English instrument makers were highly regarded as craftsmen, many defects in the construction of instruments still hampered the surveyor when he used them to survey large areas of the country. If the method of triangulation were used with a large number of triangles, the

[51] Colonel Sir Charles Close, *The Early Years of the Ordnance Survey* (Chatham, 1926), pp. 1–11; Babbage, ref. 1.

line-measuring instruments were not capable of measuring the base line with a required degree of precision so that the sides of the triangles could be calculated with reasonable accuracy. These defects were generally due to construction inaccuracies in the length of the rod, chain, or cord or to wear of the instrument during the course of the survey. On the other hand, little recognition had been given to the effect of the variation of temperature and humidity on the accuracy of line-measuring instruments.

Obstacles to the accurate measurement of angles were even greater than those to the measurement of distances. The majority of the surveyors were still using instruments with open slots for viewing the station markers. Furthermore, the circular divisions were highly inaccurate because of the method of dividing a circle, and when they were used to construct an altazimuth instrument, the design was of a crude nature. Nevertheless, at the beginning of the third quarter of the eighteenth century, instrument construction in England had developed so that a high degree of accuracy could be obtained not only in distance measurements, but for angle measurements as well.

An important invention was Dollond's achromatic lens (1758), which made possible the use of shorter refracting telescopes on surveying instruments. Likewise, the idea of placing cross hairs at right angles to each other in the field of vision of the telescope increased the accuracy with which the direction of the instrument could be aligned on distant objects. Then the construction of a dividing machine by Jesse Ramsden made possible very rapid and highly accurate division of circular and rectilinear scales. More advanced methods of machining the parts of the instruments led to sturdier instruments and thus eliminated the shake in the instruments which accounted for many errors in their operation. Finally, advances in other fields of science played a role in the search for accuracy by the surveyor.[52] There was improvement in the methods of determining heights by means of barometric pressure and also in the methods for the correction of the variations of length due to changes in temperature and humidity. We will see how important these advances were in the great triangulation survey at Hounslow Heath.

Prior to 1750 little had been accomplished in the methods of topographical surveys, except for the county and regional surveys mentioned above, and despite the need for a detailed and accurate mapping of England as a whole. The military campaigns during the rebellion in Scotland in 1746, which ended with the Battle of Culloden, played a large part in the recognition of this need. The maps used in this campaign were imperfect, being nothing more than military sketches executed with the magnetic compass and the plane table. Shortly after the rebellion, the first attempt to map the Highlands originated with Major General Watson, who began work on the project in 1747. This survey may be considered the foundation of the Ordnance Survey; Watson's project was ordered and directed by the government. General Roy, who later followed up this project, states that the work was rather crude and incomplete, for it was executed with inferior instruments of a very common sort, possibly using nothing more than the magnetic compass and the plane table. This survey was abruptly terminated by the Seven Years' War and the American Revolution.

After the close of the American Revolution, William Roy (1726–1790)[53] became interested in the work that had been organized by General Watson and, with some further

52 Close, ref. 51.
53 William Roy was a Major General of the Royal Engineers. His army engineering consisted primarily in the construction of maps and military sketches. *DNB*.

encouragement from the government, made a set of observations for a triangulation between the Observatory at Greenwich, Arthur's Seat, and Cotton Hill. In *The Early Years of the Ordnance Survey*, Colonel Close quotes from several letters of General Roy stating some of the obstacles that were encountered. Roy mentions that the Royal Astronomer, Nevil Maskelyne (1732–1811), had not completed his work on the determination of the mean density of the earth, since the Royal Astronomer had informed him that there were difficulties that hindered the work. These were the difficulties in determining by celestial observations the apparent difference of latitude of two stations on the north and south sides of a hill; in determining the distance between two parallels of latitude; and, finally, in determining the figure and dimensions of the hill. These comments by the Royal Astronomer would indicate that the geodetic surveyors were still using instruments of limited accuracy. This situation is further borne out from Roy's letters, in which he gives evidence that bearings of the type mentioned above were still being taken with the use of a magnetic compass. He further mentions that the question of a datum line had not been established.

The next impetus to topographical surveying came to England from France in 1783 when the French ambassador to England submitted a memoir of M. Cassini de Thury (1714–1784). This memoir pointed out the desirability of constructing a series of triangles from the vicinity of London to Dover, there to connect triangles with those already executed in France; the advantage of determining the relative positions of the two most famous observatories with respect to each other was thus indicated.

It was generally conceded that both topographical and geodetic surveying were in a more advanced stage of

development in France at this time than in England.[54]
Undiplomatically, this fact was hinted at in the memoir;
however, the English immediately took the challenge under
consideration, and the proposal was conveyed to the Royal
Society for consideration. From a study by the Royal
Society it was decided that the field work should be conducted by Major General Roy, financed and supported by
the government, and carried out with instruments to be
constructed by Jesse Ramsden. The final decision seems to
have been motivated by political, scientific, and practical
considerations. This decision no doubt brought about the
setting up of what is known today as the Ordnance Survey
as a branch of the English Government. The great triangulation survey at Hounslow Heath resulted from this decision.

The Great Triangulation at Hounslow Heath

Although the measurement of the base line at Hounslow
Heath and the subsequent triangulations set up on this base
line were not directly connected with land surveying, many
of the errors encountered during this operation were similar
to those of land surveying. Consequently, the methods of
correcting these errors were useful in later surveys of all
types, including land surveying. With its inherent difficulties and the extremely high degree of accuracy required
of its results, this project was probably the greatest surveying undertaking that had been accepted by any English
engineer up to that time. The operation was divided into
two parts: the choice and measurement of a base line as the
foundation of the work, and the following measurement and
calculation of the triangles whereby the base line was to be
connected with those parts of the coast adjacent to the

[54] Close, ref. 51.

French coast. After this had been done, these two sets of triangles would be connected.

Selection of the base line not only involved the choice of the base line itself but also the means and procedures of measurements. The base line was chosen on Hounslow Heath because of its proximity to London and the Royal Observatory at Greenwich, its great extent, its level surface, its lack of local obstructions in the path of the measurements, and, finally, its excellent situation as a base for further triangulation when and if needed. After the general direction had been decided, a wide path was cleared by a detachment of soldiers from the corps of engineers. In this operation, begun about 1 June 1784, an ordinary theodolite was used to give the required direction.

The second step was the preparation of the measuring instruments with the various benches, tripods, station staves, and equipment used in the measurement. For the actual measurement, Jesse Ramsden was asked to prepare a 100-foot steel chain, and the chain measurements were to be supplemented by similar measurements with deal rods.[55] The deal-rod method had been used previously in all base line surveys in other countries, and General Roy was eager to obtain the most accurate results possible. He also wished to avoid the controversy over whether the two rods should be abutted or whether matching lines on the two rods should be used. As a result of the study, the rods were constructed so that both methods could be used. Consequently, three rods were ordered to be made for the work, with an additional fourth rod to be used as the standard for comparison with the other three rods.

[55] A detailed account of the instruments used and measurements of the base line is given in William Roy, "An Account of the Measurement of a Base on Hounslow-Heath," *Philosophical Transactions*, 75 (1785), Part I, pp. 385–480 + 5 plates.

The three measuring rods, constructed of Riga wood, were 20 feet, 3 inches in length from the extremities of the bell metal tippings on their ends. They were 2 inches deep, 1½ inches broad, and were trussed both laterally and vertically so that they would be as nearly inflexible as possible. The standard rod, however, could only be trussed laterally; consequently it was made somewhat longer. Within 1½ inches of each end, a narrow piece of ivory was inlaid into the upper side of each rod. These ivory pieces were fitted with a fine black line measured accurately to exactly 20 feet, or 240 inches. The ends of the rods were machined so that they could be accurately abutted with a distance of 3 inches between the two black lines on the ivory strip of the two abutting rods.

Scale markings on the rods and the machining of the ends were executed with the greatest of precision. General Roy used his own scale of 42 inches, which had previously been divided by John Bird for Jonathan Sisson and was later owned by Graham. This scale was carefully compared with the Exchequer standard by Jesse Ramsden and found to have a high degree of accuracy. In constructing the deal rods, Ramsden made a pair of beam compasses with movable points and a micrometer to measure 20 feet. This distance was carefully laid off between the two back lines cut on the ivory strip at the ends of the rods; then, with the scale of equal parts, the bell metal tipping at the ends was ground down until any two rods would abut with 3 inches between the two lines on the ivory plates. All these measurements were again checked against the standard Exchequer yard at a fixed temperature.

It was decided that the base line distances should be measured on the horizontal rather than as slope lines. Elaborate stands, tripods, staves, and other equipment were constructed so that the work could proceed with the greatest accuracy. The whole course was first measured forward and then backward by the chain that Ramsden had previously constructed. Then the work began with the deal rods, the distances being first measured by coincidence and then by contact. In comparing the results, it was found that the method of contact was just as satisfactory as the methods of coincidence and far more rapid. A record of the temperature was kept, the lengths of the three rods were checked against the standard at morning and night, and this record was kept. It was not long before the deal rods were found to be highly unsatisfactory, because of the expansion of the rods in increased humidity. The results also showed that Riga wood expanded more than New England white pine, and further calculations showed that in the whole course the expansion might be about 2 feet in 27,406 feet.

It was then decided to discard the deal rods and use some other material. After considerable experiment, glass was decided upon, and the linear measurement was conducted with these rods. Calibration of the glass rods was as accurately determined as in the case of the wooden deal rods, but before the measurement of the base line was again started, an experiment was conducted to determine the difference of expansion in the glass rods and the steel chain that Ramsden had prepared for use in the measurements. These experiments were carried on with care and with instruments of the highest precision obtainable. The pyrometer used was one that Jesse Ramsden had improved upon for this particular experiment. The final measurements of the base line with the glass rods and steel chain were completed on 30 August 1784, and, after corrections of various sorts, the ultimate apparent length of the base line was taken as 27404.7 feet at a temperature of 62° Fahrenheit.

The measurement of the Hounslow Heath base line, with its inherent difficulties and the desire and need for an extremely high degree of accuracy, brought the development of instruments and techniques of linear measurements to possibly the highest degree of perfection yet attained. These operations indicated that highly precise linear measurements were adversely affected by many factors, the most important being the elongation of the rods due to climatic changes, in particular those of temperature and humidity. Other inaccuracies were caused by the sagging of the rods under gravity and by the wearing of the ends of the units because of the constant abutting. Another source of error was the disturbance of one unit when the next unit was brought into contact with it. A study of these and many other problems of a similar type by General Roy, Jesse Ramsden, members of various Engineering Corps, and members of the Royal Society did much to advance the ways and means of conducting measurements of length on the surface of the earth regardless of whether they were to be used in land measurement or in geodetic surveys.

Although the base line measurements of Hounslow Heath were completed in 1784, almost three years elapsed before work again began on the triangulation to connect the surveys in England with those in France. This delay was necessitated by the slow progress of Ramsden in the construction of the great theodolite to be used in the measurement of the angles in the triangulation work. During this period, however, plans were made and other apparatus constructed, stations determined, and the general plan of the work was organized so that the operation could proceed without delay once the theodolite was completed. The instrument was placed upon the first station at Hampton Poorhouse on 31 July 1787.

The theodolite (Fig. 32) constructed by Ramsden may be called an altazimuth theodolite whose telescope can be inverted on its supports, thus making it simple to adjust and

Fig. 32. The first great theodolite of Ramsden. From a photograph in Vol. 45 of the *Philosophical Transactions of the Royal Society*.

(Courtesy of the Royal Society.)

similar to other transit instruments in observatories. The instrument has a 3-foot horizontal circle made of brass, divided to 10′ and made to read to 1″ by means of two micrometer microscopes. The circle is attached by ten conical tubes, or radii, to a large vertical conical axis 24 inches in height. This axis revolves on an inner fixed axis to which the reading microscopes and leveling foot screws are fixed. A flat horizontal bar rigidly mounted across the top of the outer axis supports the telescope axis. A single vertical semicircle of 10.5 inches in diameter and divided to 30′ is fixed to the telescope and read to 5″ by means of a microscope attached to the supporting bar. The telescope axis and supporting bar are made accurately horizontal by means of two spirit levels, one 24 inches long and the other 21 inches long. There were two achromatic telescopes, each of 36 inches focal length, with double object glasses of 2½ inches aperture. The erecting eyepiece magnifies 54 diameters, but other eyepieces were used at various times. The telescope diaphragm has fixed cross wires and a horizontal traveling wire controlled by a micrometer screw. It could be illuminated through the horizontal axis of rotation for night work. There are clamps and tangent screws for fine adjustments fitted to the horizontal and vertical axes. This theodolite and another of similar construction (Fig. 33), completed about 1790, were in constant use until 1862. During the principal triangulation of Great Britain and Ireland, sights were taken over 100 miles distance. The probable error of a single observation with the above-described instrument was about 5″ for a distance of 70 miles.

As the work of measuring the triangles progressed, it was decided to set up a base of verification in Romney Marsh. Since the steel chain of Ramsden had shown such a consistently high degree of accuracy when compared with the measurement of Hounslow Heath base line by the glass rods, it was decided to use the chain with extreme care in measur-

Fig. 33. The second great theodolite of Ramsden. Photograph
from the Science Museum, South Kensington, London.
(Courtesy of the Director. Crown copyright reserved.)

184

ing the verification base.[56] The completed work showed an error of about 1 part in 28,000 in the measurement of the Hounslow Heath base line. The final calculation of the series of 45 triangles extending from Windsor to Dunkirk, where they connected with the series of triangles extending from Paris to the same point, showed remarkable results with respect to the accuracy of the measurements and calculations of the whole project. The base line at Dunkirk, when computed by the French system of triangles, showed an error of only 15 inches from that calculated from the Hounslow Heath base line.

Summary and Conclusions

The close of the eighteenth century brings us to the end of our story. We have witnessed the slow but gradual development of English land surveying from crude instruments and primitive methods to a highly accurate scientific art. This development was accomplished by many people and over almost two thousand years.

English land surveying actually begins with the introduction into Britain by the Saxons of the open-field system of agriculture and land tenure. The Saxons also brought with them a system of land measures which were adapted to suit the conditions in England and modified to suit their needs. Many of these measures were later approved by statute and are still being used at the present time.

With the conquest of England by the Normans, the system of agriculture and types of land tenure began to

[56] A detailed account of the survey on the base line of Hounslow Heath and a description of Ramsden's great theodolite is given in "An Account of the Trigonometric Operation, Whereby the Distance Between the Meridians of the Royal Observatories of Greenwich and Paris have been Determined by Major-General William Roy," *Philosophical Transactions*, 80 (1790), Part I, pp. 111–270 + 11 plates.

change. By the close of the fifteenth century the general intellectual and economic level of society in England had risen, and as a result there were greater demands on agriculture. This eventually led to a gradual breakdown of the system of scattered land holdings and the beginning of enclosure of the open fields and common lands. This new system of landholding required a greater number of trained land measurers.

In the early part of the sixteenth century, the land steward, with his role as a land measurer, grew in importance. Two texts, the first to be written in English, appeared; one dealing with the duties of the land steward, the other with the duties and practices of the land measurer.

During the second half of the sixteenth century the scientific growth of the art of surveying began to take form and a number of important works on scientific subjects closely related to surveying appeared. Outstanding among these were the writings of Leonard and Thomas Digges. These writings gave a wealth of information on existing instruments and suggestions for the constructions of new instruments. Important among the new instruments was the theodelitus, an instrument of great significance to English surveying. During this period there also arose a distinguished group of instrument designers, makers, and mathematical practitioners. Prominent among this group was Humphrey Cole, the craftsman of the first English theodolite.

Throughout the sevententh century there were a number of distinguished writers, among them being Rathborne and Leybourn. Important new methods were practiced at this time, including the use of backsighting and the traverse method of surveying an enclosure. The circumferentor was introduced in surveying practice, double sights were attached to the instruments, and the ball-and-socket was added to the tripod, which had been introduced earlier in the century. The notebook was utilized in the field work, and trigonometry was used in some calculations.

In the seventeenth century there were also a number of new inventions, which played a significant role in instrument construction during the eighteenth century. Of special interest were the vernier for reading circular and rectangular scales, the telescope, the micrometer, and the idea of placing cross hairs in the focal plane of the telescope. These inventions and the developments of instrument construction of the preceding century were applied to the construction of new instruments in the first half of the eighteenth century. By mid-century, hand dividing of instrument scales had reached its peak under Sisson, Bird, and others. This method was difficult, tedious, and expensive. After various attempts a satisfactory method of mechanically dividing scales was devised by Jesse Ramsden. Throughout the century the practice of surveying improved and the recognition and correction of errors were advanced. Calculations were improved by a greater use of trigonometry and the method of double areas.

Although not directly related to land surveying, the construction of the instruments, the field operations, and the final calculations of the great triangulation survey at Hounslow Heath were of great importance. The solution of the problems involved and the success of the operations advanced the practices of all types of surveying through the nineteenth and into the twentieth century.

At the opening of the nineteenth century, the theory and practice of surveying were well established and instrument construction had reached a high degree of perfection. The way was now opened for the instrument makers to exert their efforts in the construction of smaller, compact instruments with a high degree of accuracy. As these instruments were standardized in manufacture, the cost of production decreased to the point where they were available to the average land surveyor. At the same time, the increase in the number of technical schools giving courses directly related to surveying taught practicing surveyors to conduct their surveys with a high degree of accuracy. Finally, the development of a mathematical theory of errors and adjustment of observations was a great aid to the surveyor in his search for and adjustment of the errors in his survey.

At the close of the eighteenth century, the basic rules and laws governing the methods of surveying had been established on a sound scientific basis. Surveying practices changed but little from these rules and laws over the next century. In instrument construction the basic principles had been worked out, and from then on there was only the problem of modifying these instruments to meet the needs of special problems that presented themselves. Methods used in conducting large geodetic surveys changed only with the problems at hand. The history of nearly all geodetic linear measurements over the next century is similar to that of the base line measurement at Hounslow Heath.

In the twentieth century the addition of photographic and electronic equipment to some form of the existing instruments brought about many changes in the surveying of large geographical areas. However, in the surveys of small enclosures and tracts of land, surveyors today still employ the same basic principles of survey and instruments as those in use at the close of the eighteenth century.

Selected Bibliography

Bibliographical Works

Clark, Ernest. "Early Books on Agriculture," Discussion of paper at February meeting, *Transactions of Bibliographical Society, 3* (1929), 160–162. In the discussion of this paper mention was made of the evidence in support of John Fitzherbert's claim to the authorship of the books on *Husbandry* and *Surveying*, usually credited to Anthony Fitzherbert.

Fitzherbert, Reginald F. C. "The Authorship of the 'Book of Husbandry and the Book of Surveying,'" *English Historical Review, 12* (1897), 225–236. A paper attempting to prove that John Fitzherbert instead of Anthony was the author of the book on *Surveying* and *Husbandry*.

Gay, Edwin F. "The Authorship of the 'Book of Husbandry' and the 'Book of Surveying,'" *Quarterly Journal of Economics, 18* (1904), 588–590. The author of this paper presents conclusive evidence that the author of the two books was John Fitzherbert instead of Anthony.

Karpinski, Louis. *Bibliography of Mathematical Works Printed in America Through 1850* (Ann Arbor, 1940), p. 10. This excellent bibliography contains 902 entries pertaining to mathematics and related subjects. Texts on surveying are included among these entries.

Karpinski, L. C. "Biographical Check List of all Works on Trigonometry Published up to 1700 A.D.," *Scripta Mathematica*, 12 (1924), 267–283. A bibliography of the works on trigonometry published throughout the world before 1700.

Pollard, Alfred W., and Redgrave, G. R. *A Short Title Catalogue of Books Printed in England, Scotland and Ireland and British Books Printed Abroad, 1475–1640* (London. 1926). An excellent catalogue of early works on English surveying.

Taylor, E. G. R. *Tudor Geography 1485–1583* (London, 1930), pp. 144–148. A treatise on the mathematical practitioners and their works from 1485 to 1583.

Taylor, E. G. R. *The Mathematical Practitioners of Tudor and Stuart England* (Cambridge, 1954). This outstanding work on Tudor and Stuart mathematical practitioners is divided into three parts. Part I gives the contributions and narrative of the practitioners from 1485 to 1715; Part II gives biographical notes on the practitioners; Part III lists the publications with notes on the practitioners.

History: General

Bennett, H. S. *Life on the English Manor* (New York, 1937).

Beresford, Maurice. *The Lost Villages of England* (London, 1954). An excellent discussion of early land tenure and enclosing in England through the Anglo-Norman period.

Bogart, Ernest L. *Economic History of Europe 1760–1939* (New York, 1942), pp. 1–150.

Cam, Helen. *England Before Elizabeth* (London, 1950). A concise, authoritative history of England from the Roman occupation to Elizabeth I with emphasis on the economic and political development during the Anglo-Norman period.

Cheyney, Edward P., ed. *English Manorial Documents* (London, 1885). Translations and reprints from the "Original Sources of European History," Vol. 3, No. 5. This text gives numerous translations of the proceedings of courts of survey and the surveyor's inventories of English manors.

Chiera, Edward. *They Wrote on Clay* (Chicago, 1938). A history of the Sumerians obtained from the inscriptions on their clay tablets. Chiera gives examples of the records of land measuring found on some of these tablets.

Chronicon Monasterii de Abington (London, 1958), Vol. 1, pp. 58–59. The Chronicles of the Monastery of Abington give descriptions of early land holdings during the late Saxon and early Anglo-Norman periods.

Collingwood, R. G., and Myres, J. N. L. *Roman Britain and the English Settlements* (Oxford, 1949). A discussion of Britain at the close of the Roman occupation and the coming of the Saxon invaders.

Fitzherbert, Anthony. *The Book of Husbandry*, edited with introduction, notes, and glossary by Rev. Walter Skeat (London, 1882). An early sixteenth-century work giving instructions to the lord of the manor on the proper management of the manor. The rights and duties of the lord with respect to his tenants are definitely defined as well as those of the tenant with respect to his lord.

Gray, H. L. *English Field Systems* (Cambridge, 1915). A study of early English field system and the distribution of the arable land among the tenants.

Hart, W. H., ed. *Historia et Cartularium Monasterii Saneti Gloucestriae* (London, 1863–1867), Vol. 1. This monastic history gives many details of the boundaries of the lands controlled by the monasteries in Gloucestershire.

Loret, Victor. "Les Grandes Inscriptions de Mes à Saqqarah," *Zeitschrift für Aegyptische Sprache*, 49 (1901), 1–10. A discussion of the inscriptions at Saqqarah giving evidence of the practice of surveying by the Egyptians.

Myers A. R. *England in the Late Middle Ages* (Harmondsworth, 1952).

Orwin, C. S. and C. S. *The Open Fields* (Oxford, 1954). Discussion of the methods of plowing in Saxon England and its effect on the division of the arable land.

Poole, Austin. *Medieval England* (Oxford, 1958), Vol. 2. A general history of medieval England with sections on farming and land tenure.

Prothero, Roland E. *English Farming Past and Present* (London, 1912). An authoritative work on English farming, land tenure, and enclosing.

Rolls of Parliament (1502), Vol. 5, p. 591. References to the Saxon and early Anglo-Norman units of land measures.

Vinogradoff, P. *The Growth of the Manor* (London, 1905).

History: Mathematics, Science, and Technology

Babbage, Charles. *Reflections on the Decline of Science in England* (London, 1830). A general discussion of the condition of science in England from the death of Newton through 1850.

Braunmühl, A von. *Vorlesungen über die Geschichte der Trigonometrie* (Leipzig, 1900). History of trigonometry in two volumes from the ancients through the nineteenth century.

Clavius, Christopher. *Operum Mathematicorum* (Magvntiae, 1611), Vol. 3. This work discusses many topics on mathematical instruments. The division of scales by transversals is considered.

Crombie, A. C. *History of Science* (London, 1952).

Darby, H. C. "The Agrarian Contribution to Surveying in England," *The Geographical Journal, 82* (1933), pp. 529–538.

Grant, Robert. *History of Physical Astronomy* (London, 1852). A discussion of the use of Gascoigne's micrometer is given in this text.

Gunther, R. T. *Early Science at Oxford* (Oxford, 1922), Vol. 2. A study of the development of mathematics and science at Oxford in the sixteenth and seventeenth centuries.

Halliwell, J. O. *A Collection of Letters of the Progress of Science in England* (London, 1841). Letters from numerous English scientists describing the progress of science in England.

Haskins, C. H. *Studies in the History of Science* (Cambridge, 1924).

Hinkle, William J. *A New Boundary Stone of Nebuchadnezzar I* (Philadelphia, 1907), pp. 116–160. The publication gives a translation of the inscription on a boundary stone which is the records of a survey in the time of Nebuchadnezzar I, about 1400 B.C. This stone is in the collection of the Museum at the University of Pennsylvania.

Howland, Arthur C. "The Institutional Pattern of the Middle Ages: Inheritance and Legacy," *University of Pennsylvania Bicentennial Conference* (Philadelphia, 1941), pp. 60–75. A lecture given at the University of Pennsylvania in 1941 on the contributions of Eastern science and culture to modern civilization.

Johnson, Francis R. *Astronomical Thought in Renaissance England* (Baltimore, 1937).

Kästner, A. G. *Geschichte der Mathematik* (Göttingen, 1796–1800). History of mathematics with special references to mathematical instruments and their construction.

Needham, Joseph. *Science and Civilization in China* (Cambridge, 1959), Vol. 3. Volume 3 discusses the use of the magnetic compass for cartographic surveying by the Chinese during the eleventh century.

Neugebauer, Otto. "Exact Science in Antiquity," *University of Pennsylvania Bicentennial Conference* (Philadelphia, 1941) pp. 23–31. A lecture on ancient science given at the University of Pennsylvania in 1941.

Repsold, Johannes A. *Zur Geschichte der astronomischen Messwerkzeuge von Puerbach bis Reichenbach 1450–1830* (Leipzig, 1908). A comprehensive study of astronomical measuring instruments and their uses.

Sarton, George. *Ancient Science and Modern Civilization* (Lincoln, 1924). A survey in three lectures of the world of Hellenism from its beginning in the ninth century B.C. to the fifth century A.D. and its influence on modern civilization.

Sarton, George. *Introduction to the History of Science* (Baltimore, 1927–1947), 3 vols. An outstanding pioneering study of the history of science from the ancients to the fourteenth century.

Sarton, George. "The First Explanation of Decimal Fractions and Measures (1585)," *Isis*, 23 (1938), 152–244.

Singer, Charles *et al.*, eds. *A History of Technology* (Oxford, 1954–1958), 5 vol. This is a series of outstanding volumes in the history of technology from the earliest times through 1900.

Smith, David Eugene. *History of Mathematics* (Boston, 1923–1925), 2 vols. An authoritative work on the history of elementary mathematics. Volume 1 gives a general survey of elementary mathematics, while Volume 2 gives a topical analysis.

Thevénot, Melchisédech. *Discours sur l'Art de Navigation* (Paris, 1681). A description of the bubble spirit level.

Thureau-Dangin, François. "Un Cadastre Chaldéen," *Revue d'
Assyrologie et d'Archéologie Orientale, 4* (1897), 13–20.
This paper gives evidence from several tablets that some
form of surveying was practiced by the Chaldeans at an
early date.

Winter, H. J. J. *Eastern Science: An Outline of its Scope and
Contributions* (London, 1952). A study of the spread of
Eastern science in the Middle Ages and its impact upon
modern civilization.

Woodbury, Robert S. *History of the Gear-Cutting Machine*
(Cambridge, 1958). An authoritative study of the history
of gear-cutting machines. Slight references to the clockmakers and the work of Ramsden.

Wolf, A. *A History of Science, Technology and Philosophy
in the 16th and 17th Centuries* (New York, 1939). An
authoritative work on the history of science and technology
in the sixteenth and seventeenth centuries.

Instruments

Adams, George. *Geometrical and Graphical Essays* (London,
1797).

Apian, Peter. *Instrument-Buch* (Ingolstadt, 1533). Concise description of sixteenth-century instrument construction in
Europe.

Auzout, A. "Manière Exacte Pour Prendre le Diamètre des
Planètes," *Histoire de l'académie royale des sciences depuis
1666 jusqu'à 1699* (Paris, 1773), Vol. 3, pp. 118–130. A description of the astronomical micrometer developed by
Auzout and Picard.

Bell, Louis. *The Telescope* (New York, 1922). This work traces
the development of the telescope and gives the names of
many who contributed to its development.

*Catalogue of the Collection of the Science Museum of South
Kensington—Geodesy and Surveying,* compiled by E. Lancaster-Jones (London, 1925). A descriptive catalogue of
surveying and geodetic instruments in the Science Museum,
South Kensington, London.

Chaulnes, M. le Duc de. *Nouvelle méthode pour diviser les
instruments de mathématiques et d' astronomie* (Paris,

1768). A work of the Duc de Chaulnes giving his methods of dividing mathematical instruments with cuts illustrating the instruments.

Coggeshall, Henry. *The Art of Practical Measuring* (London, 1722). A description of many instruments and their use in all types of measurements.

Court, T., and von Rohr, M. "A History of the Telescope," *Transactions of the Optical Society, 30* (1929), 207–260; *32* (1931), 113–122.

Cunningham, William. *Cosmographicall Glasse* (London, 1559). A comprehensive work on the various branches of mathematical practice but little on surveying. There is a line drawing of his instrument, the "cosmographicall glasse."

Derham, W. "Extract from Mr. Gascoigne and Mr. Crabtrie Letters Proving that Mr. Gascoigne to have been the Inventor of Telescopic Sights of Mathematical Instruments and not the French," *Philosophical Transactions of the Royal Society of London, 30* (1750), 603–610. These letters give conclusive evidence that Gascoigne developed and used his micrometer in astronomical work before the French.

Digges, Thomas. *Alae seu Scalae Mathematicae* (London, 1573). This publication has little to say of surveying, but there is a discussion of diagonal scales with drawing illustrating several types of such scales.

Drachmann, A. G. "Hero's Instruments," *History of Technology*, ed. by Charles Singer *et al.* (Oxford, 1957), Vol. 3. Drachmann describes the surveying instruments of Hero and gives a drawing of his dioptra and level.

Dreyer, F. L. E. "On the Invention of the Sextant," *Astronomische Nachrichten, 115* (1886), 31–35. A discussion of the invention of the sextant and its uses in astronomy.

Gardiner, William. *See* Surveying.

Green, William. *Description and Use of an Improved Refracting Telescope with Scale for Surveying* (London, 1778). The first English description of the construction of the stadia for measuring distances with the theodolite.

Gunter, Edmund. *The Works of Edmund Gunter*, 4th ed. (London, 1662). *The Works of Gunter* gives descriptions and uses of the devices and tables which are credited to the author. Gunter is best known to the practicing surveyor for the surveying chain which bears his name.

Gunter, Siegmund. *Die Erfindung des Baculum Geometricus Bibliotheca Mathematica* (1885), Vol. 2. Some discussion of the divisions of circular scales by transversals.

Gunther, R. T. "The Astrolabe: Its Uses and Derivatives," *The Scottish Geographical Magazine, 27* (1927), 135–147. A discussion of the various uses of the astrolabes devised by sixteenth-century instrument makers.

Gunther, R. T. "Digges' Theodelitus, The First Booke of the Pantometria," *Old Ashmolean Reprints IV* (Oxford, 1927), Preface. A detailed description of the theodelitus and topographical instrument of Leonard Digges.

Gunther, R. T. *Early Science in Cambridge* (Oxford, 1937). A study of sixteenth-century science at Cambridge University with references to mathematical instruments.

Gunther, R. T. "The Great Astrolabe and Other Scientific Instruments of Humphrey Cole," *Archaelogia, 29,* 2nd ser. (1929), 273–317. An explanation of the great astrolabe and other instruments constructed by Humphrey Cole. Gunther states that many of these principles could have been used by Cole in constructing the theodolite.

Haskold, H. D. "Remarks Upon Surveying Instruments," *Transactions American Institute of Mining Engineers, 31* (1902), 76 ff. A discussion of the influence of the development of surveying instruments on the development of mining instruments.

Hopton, Arthur. *See* Surveying.

Howe, Charles S. "Early History of Instruments and the Art of Observing in Astronomy and Civil Engineering," *Journal of Associated Engineering Societies, 18* (1897), 170 ff.

Kiely, Edmond R. *Surveying Instruments* (New York, 1947). An authoritative history of the development of surveying instruments from the ancients through the Renaissance period.

Klingenstierna, S. "Anmerkung über des Gesetz der Brechung der Lichtstrahlen von Verchiedener Art," *Der Königlisch–Schwedischen Akademie der Wissenchaften Abhandlungen, 10* (1733), 300–309. This paper discusses the progress being made in constructing an achromatic lens by showing that with glass and water there could be color without refraction.

La Hire, Philippe de. *L'Ecole des Arpenteurs* (Paris, 1689). The text gives a discussion of water levels that had been in use for at least two centuries.

Lancaster–Jones, E. "Criticism of Heron's Dioptra," *The Geographical Journal, 69* (1927), 140. This paper tends to prove that according to Schone's description of Hero's dioptra it would be impossible to construct such an instrument.

Leroy, Julien. *Règle Artificielle du Temps, Traité* (Paris, 1737). A study of the construction of notched wheels in clocks.

Lucar, Cyprian. *See* Surveying.

Ludlum, W. "An Introduction and Notes on Mr. Bird's Method of Dividing," *Philosophical Transactions, 99* (1800), Part I, pp. 105–143. A description of Bird's method of hand dividing circular scales.

Muirhead, James Patrick. *The Origin and Progress of the Mechanical Inventions of James Watt* (London, 1854), Vol. 1. A catalogue and description of the inventions of James Watt. In particular a description of Watt's application of the stadia in measuring distances.

Neckham, Alexander. *De Naturis Rerum*, ed. by Thomas Wright (London, 1863), pp. I–XXXVII, and 98–102. Probably the first European reference to the nautical use of the magnetic needle was given in this work by Neckham.

Nuñez, Pedro. *De Grepusculis Liber Unus* (Lisbon, 1542). In this work Nuñez gives a description and method of constructing the nonius.

Ramsden, Jesse. *Description of an Engine for the Division of Mathematical Instruments*, published by order of the Commissioners of Longitude (London, 1777). This pamphlet gives a description of Ramsden's engine for dividing mathematical instruments. There is also a description of his screw-cutting machine.

Robertson, John. *A Treatise of Such Mathematical Instruments as are Usually Put into a Portable Case* (London, 1747). A description of the usual instruments carried in a portable case by a mathematical practitioner.

Salmoiraghi, Angelo. *Istrumenti e Metodi Moderni di Geometria Applicata* (Milano, 1884), Vol. 1, Part I. Possibly the first description of the construction and use of a form of the stadia.

Schone, Herman. "Die Dioptra des Herons," *Archäologisches Institut des Deutschen Reichs, 16* (1900). A description and reconstruction of Hero's dioptra.

Scott, Dunbar. "Mine Surveying Instruments," *Institution of Mining Engineers, 23* (1881–1882). A discussion of the influence of the development of the theodolite on the development of mining instruments.

Smeaton, John. "Observations on the Graduations of Astronomical Instruments," *Royal Society of London. Philosophical Transactions, 76* (1786), 1–47. This paper, among other things, gives Smeaton's criticism of Bird's hand method of dividing mathematical and astronomical instruments.

Smith, R. *Compleat System of Optics* (London, 1738), Vol. 2. This text on optics gives the first exact and definite information on the method of hand dividing mathematical instruments in the eighteenth century.

Stevenson, Thomas. "Some Account of Leveling Instruments," *Journal of the Franklin Institute, 8,* 3rd ser. (1884), 217 ff. A discussion of the lapse of time before the spirit, bubble level came into use as a part of leveling instruments.

Stone, Edward Noble. "Roman Surveying Instruments," *University of Washington Publications, 4* (1928), 215–248. A study of Roman surveying instruments with reference to parts of instruments recovered from excavations at Mt. Vesuvius.

Taylor, E. G. R. "The Plane Table in the Sixteenth Century," *The Geographical Magazine, 45* (1929), 205–211. A paper describing the invention of the plane table and its operation during the sixteenth century.

Thiout, Antoine, *Traité d'Horlogerie* (Paris, 1741), Vol. 2, pp. 327–400. A study of the development of the mechanisms of clocks.

Thompson, Sylvanus P. "The Rose of the Winds; The Origin and Development of the Compass Card," *Proceedings of the British Academy* (London, 1913–1914). A study of the origin and development of the compass card, the division of the card into points, the wind roses, and the use of the fleur-de-lis.

Troughton, Edward. "An Account of the Method of Dividing Astronomical and Other Instruments," *Philosophical Trans-*

actions, 109 (1809), 105–143. An account of Troughton's method to correct some of the faults in Bird's methods of dividing mathematical instruments. Bird's method had been previously criticized by Smeaton.

Vernier, Pierre. *La construction, l'usage et les propriétés de quadrant nouveau de mathématique* (Brussels, 1631). This treatise gives a description of a method of dividing and reading scales which were later named "the vernier."

Watkins, J. Elfreth. "The Ramsden Dividing Engine," *Annual Report of the Smithsonian Institution* (Washington, 1891). This report gives a description of Ramsden's dividing engine and its acquisition by the Smithsonian Institution.

Wellisch, Sigmund. "Die Erfindung der Triangulierung," *Zeitschrift des Oesterr. Ingenieur- und Architekten-Vereines, 20* (1899), 355 ff. An attempt to prove that August Hirschvogel was using a highly developed method of surveying by triangulation during the first half of the sixteenth century.

Winter, Heinrich. "What is the Present Stage of Research in Regard to the Development of the Compass in Europe?" *Research and Progress, 2* (1936), 225–233. A review of the research on the magnetic compass from the latter part of the nineteenth century through the first quarter of the twentieth century.

Surveying: Texts and Methods

Agas, Ralph. *A Preparative to Plotting of Lands and Tenementes for Surveighs* (London, 1596). In this text the plane table and theodolite of Digges are suggested for use in the surveys. Agas was one of the first to suggest the use of Digges' theodolite.

Atwell, John. *The Faithful Surveyor* (London, 1658). The first text of the seventeenth century to suggest that surveying with the chain only could be done as accurately and more quickly than with angle-measuring instruments.

Barthelet, Thomas. *Here beginneth a ryght fruteful mater. & hathe to name the boke of Surveynge and Improuementes* (London, 1545). The title page of this publication carries the name Thomas Barthelet, but the text is almost identical with that of the *Book of Surveying* of Master Fitzherbert.

199

Benese, Richard. *This Boke sheweth the maner of measurynge of all maner of land* . . . (Southwark, 1537). The second text on surveying printed in English. It gives the surveyor definite rules and instructions for the conduct of the survey with tables and rules for calculating the areas of the parcels of land.

Blume, F., Lachmann, K., and Rudorff, A. *Die Schriften der Romischen Feldmesser* (Berlin, 1848). Useful in the study of Roman surveying but should be used with care.

Bourne, William. *A Book Called the Treasure for Travellers* (London, 1578). The text was partly drawn from a manuscript previously written for presentation to Lord Birghley. There is a discussion on surveying.

Burgh, Thomas. *A Method to Determine the Area of Right-lined Figures Universally* (London, 1724). A pamphlet giving the first description in English of the determination of the area of an irregular figure by the method of double areas.

Burns, Arthur. *Geodaesia Improved: or a New and Correct Method of Surveying Made Exceedingly Easy* (Chester, 1776). Although Burns' method of surveying is primarily by chain only, the text is important for its discussion of the errors in the survey and the rights of the landowner and the tenant.

Close, Colonel Sir Charles. *The Early Years of the Ordnance Survey* (Chatham, 1926). A discussion of the difficulties encountered in establishing the English Ordnance Survey.

Davis, William A. *Complete Treatise on Land Surveying by the Chain, Cross, and Offset Staffs Only* (London, 1798).

Digges, Leonard. *A Booke Named Tectonicon* (London, 1556). One of the first texts to give a general discussion of geometrical surveying with simple instruments which could be constructed by a skilled surveyor. These instruments included the geometrical square, the cross-staff, the carpenter's square, and others.

Digges, Leonard. *A Geometrical Treatise Named Pantometria* (London, 1571). This work is a comprehensive study of the uses of mathematical instruments including the topographical instrument embodying the theodolite.

Emerson, William. *The Art of Surveying or Measuring Land* (London, 1770). The text outlines a suggested course of study for prospective surveyors with comments on their training.

Eyre, John. *The Exact Surveyor* (London, 1654). Eyre's work is the first seventeenth-century text to attempt a comprehensive discussion of the errors of the survey.

Fitzherbert, Master. *Here Begynneth a right Frutefull Mater: and hath to name the boke Surveynge and Improvementes* (Londini, 1523). The first text on surveying printed in English. This work is concerned primarily with the duties of the land steward in the operation of the manor. A small portion of the work is devoted to land measuring.

Gardiner, William. *Practical Surveying Improved: or Land Measuring According to the Most Correct Methods* (London, 1737). An important feature of this text is a detailed description of Sisson's improved theodolite.

Gardner, Alan H. "The Inscriptions of Mes," *Untersuchungen zur Altertumskunde Aegyptens, 4* (1915), pp. 1–51. An account of some of the early inscriptions of the Egyptians relating to surveying and the results of the surveys.

Gibson, Robert. *A Treatise on Land Surveying* (Dublin, 1739). A popular text on surveying published in the mid-eighteenth century. This was the first English surveying text to be published in the North American colonies.

Gibson, Robert. *A Treatise of Practical Surveying* (Philadelphia, 1785). First English surveying text to be published in the North American colonies. It passed through twenty-one American editions.

Gray, John. *The Art of Land-Measuring Explained* (Glasgow, 1737).

Hammond, John. *The Practical Surveyor* (London, 1731). Although the title page carries the name of John Hammond, the text was probably written by Samuel Cunn.

Hopton, Arthur. *Speculum Topographicum: or the Topographicall Glasses* (London, 1611). This treatise is important in that it gives the first detailed description of the instruments available for use by seventeenth-century surveyors; it shows the adaptation of the particular instrument to the need of the surveyor, it provides detailed instruction for the use of triangulation, and it suggests the use of logarithms in calculations.

Lawrence, Edward. *The Young Surveyor's Guide: or a New Introduction to the Whole Art of Land Surveying* (London, 1721). A standard text on surveying, but it does give a line drawing of Sisson's improved theodolite.

Leigh, Valentine. *The Most Profitable and Commendable Science of Surveying of Landes, Tenemens, and Hereditamentes* (London, 1577). Although the methods of geometrical surveying had come into use, the author still wrote on surveying after the manner of Fitzherbert.

Leybourn, William. *Pantometria, or the Whole Art of Surveying* (London, 1650). A short treatise on surveying by Leybourn published before the *Compleat Surveyor.*

Leybourn, William. *The Compleat Surveyor: Containing the Whole Art of Surveying of Land* (London, 1653). One of the outstanding texts of the eighteenth century. Leybourn's works exerted a greater influence on the practicing surveyor than any other writer of the seventeenth century.

Love, John. *Geodaesia: or the Art of Surveying and Measuring of Land Made Easie* (London, 1688). A popular work which was written, according to Love, for the use of young surveyors in the North American colonies where conditions were much different from those in England.

Lucar, Cyprian. *A Treatise Named Lucar Solace* (London, 1590). Lucar's text is essentially a text on surveying with the plane table only. There are line drawings and a discussion of the instruments available for the surveyor's use.

Lyons, Sir Henry G. "Ancient and Modern Land Measurements," *The Geographical Teacher, 13* (1925), 425–432.

Martindale, Adam. *The Country-Survey-Book: or Land-Meter's Vademecum* (London, 1682). This text was apparently popular and widely used by surveyors. Martindale suggests that the surveyor construct his own instruments in a "do-it-yourself" manner.

Middleton, Reginald, and Chadwick, Osbert. *A Treatise on Surveying*, ed. by W. Fisher Cassie, 6th ed. (New York, 1956), 2 vols. A two-volume edition of a standard English work on modern land surveying.

Noble, Benjamin. *Geodaesia Hibernica or an Essay on Practical Surveying* (Dublin, 1763).

Price, Derek J. "Medieval Land Surveying and Topographical Maps," *The Geographical Journal, 121* (1955), 1–10. A study of the survey map of Wildmore Fen. This is probably one of the earliest examples of an English map with North at the top.

Rathborne, Aaron. *The Surveyor in Foure Bookes* (London, 1616). The first full-scale work on geometrical surveying which embodies the recent advances in surveying methods. Rathborne describes his new decimal chain, his note book, and discusses the uses of the peractor, theodolite, and circumferentor. This work was highly regarded by seventeenth-century surveyors.

Roy, William. "An Account of the Measurement of a Base on Hounslow-Heath," *Philosophical Transactions*, 75 (1785), Part I, pp. 385–480 + 5 Plates. A detailed account of the operations of the survey at Hounslow Heath. Also a description and discussion of the instruments used in this survey.

Roy, William. "An Account of the Trigonometric Operation, Whereby the Distance Between the Meridians of the Royal Observatories of Greenwich and Paris have been Determined by Major-General William Roy," *Philosophical Transactions, 80* (1790), Part I, pp. 111–270 + 11 plates. A detailed description of the office work of the survey of the base at Hounslow Heath with the final results of this survey.

Sturmy, Samuel. *Mathematical and Practical Arts* (London, 1669), Vol. 5.

Talbot, Benjamin. *The Compleat Art of Land-Measuring or a Guide to Practical Surveying* (London, 1780). Use of the catoptric sextant as an angle-measuring instrument is explained in this text.

Taylor, E. G. R. "The Earliest Account of Triangulation," *Scottish Geographical Magazine, 43* (1927), 341–345. An account of the method of surveying by triangulation proposed by Gemma Frisius.

Webb, Bernard. "An Early Map and Description of the Inquest on Wildmore Fen in the Twelfth Century," *Lincoln Architectural and Archaeological Reports and Papers, 2* (1944), 141–156. This map is probably the first English map with North at the top.

Wilson, Henry. *Geodaesia Catenea: or Surveying by the Chain Only* (London, 1732), A standard eighteenth-century text on surveying. However, Gray is the first author to suggest Burgh's double-area method of casting up the area of an irregular piece of land.

Worsop, Edward. *A Discoverie of Sundrie Errours and Faults Daily Committed by Landemeaters* (London, 1582). First English text on surveying to point out the errors committed by the surveyors and to argue for an organization to examine and license surveyors for practice.

Measures

Ault, Warren Ortman, *Private Jurisdiction in England* (New Haven, 1923). Useful in the study of English laws relating to the early surveyor and his relation to the manor.

Berryman, A. E. *Historical Metrology* (London, 1953). Studies the rise of measures from the ancients to the present with references to the acre.

Chisholm, H. W. *On the Science of Weighing and Measuring* (London, 1877).

Coverdale Bible, I Samuel XV, 14. Reference to the acre as a unit of length.

Nicholson, Edward. *Men and Measures* (London, 1912). A general discussion of weights and measures with particular reference to the "rod length" used in England and the acres derived from these measures.

Pickering, Darby. *The Statutes at Large* (Cambridge, 1762). Volume 1 gives a discussion of many of the laws pertaining to early English weights and measures.

Stubbs, John. *The Discovery of Gaping Gulf* (London, 1579). Discussion of the use of the term "rod" as a unit of measure of area as well as a unit of length.

Thorpe, B. *Ancient Laws and Institutions of England* (London, 1840). A discussion of the statutes standardizing weights and measures in England.

Watson, C. M. *British Weights and Measures* (London, 1910). A standard work on English weights and measures with emphasis on measures of length.

Woodhouse, W. S. B. *Measures, Weights, and Monies of All Nations* (London, 1890).

Biography

Aubrey, John. *Brief Lives* (Oxford, 1898). A useful biographical list of important Englishmen of the fifteenth and sixteenth centuries.

Bibliotheca Britannico-Hibernica Thomas Tannero. Episcopo Asaphenesi (London, 1748). Early English and Irish biography.

Dictionary of National Biography (Oxford, 1885–1939). An outstanding English biography from early times through 1930.

Fasti Ecclesiae Anglicanae (Oxford, 1885), Vol. 1 and Vol. 2. Early English Biography.

Foster, Joseph. *Alumni Oxonienses* (London, 1891), Vol. 1. A biographical list of early alumni of Oxford University.

Grainger, J. *Biographical History of England*, 3rd ed. (London, 1799).

Hellman, C. Doris. "John Bird, Mathematical Instrument Maker in the Strand," *Isis*, *17* (1932), 127–152.

Johnson, Francis "Letter to the Editor," *The Times Literary Supplement* (London, 5 April 1934). A note to the editor of the London *Times Literary Supplement* in an attempt to clear up several controversial events in the life of Leonard Digges.

Le Neve, John. *Monumenta Anglicana* (London, 1719). Consists primarily of biographical notes taken from English monuments.

Parkinson, Richard, ed. *The Life of Adam Martindale*, written by himself. Printed for the Chatham Society (London, 1845). An autobiography of Adam Martindale in which he discusses his training as a surveyor.

Patterson, Louise Diehl. "Leonard and Thomas Digges. Biographical Notes," *Isis*, *42* (1952), 120–121.

Rose, Hugh James. *New Biographical Dictionary* (London, 1850).

Smith, David Eugene. *See* History, Mathematics.

Taylor, E. G. R. *See* Bibliographical Works.

Taylor, E. G. R. "William Bourne: A Chapter in Tudor Geography," *The Geographical Journal*, *72* (1928), 329–341. The biography of William Bourne with a discussion of his method on triangulation.

Trusdale, W. A. "The First Engineer," *Journal Association of Engineering Societies*, *19* (1897), 1 ff. A biographical sketch of Hero of Alexandria.

Education

Barker, Ernest. *British Universities* (London, 1946).

Bretnor, Thomas. *A Newe Almanacke for 1616* (London, 1616), p. 6. An advertisement in the almanac gives the list of subjects taught by Bretnor to prospective surveyors.

Kokomoor, F. W. "The Distinctive Seventeenth Century Geometry," *Isis, 10* (1923), 367–415.

Pope, Walter. *Life of Right Reverend Seth, Lord Bishop of Salisbury* (London, 1697). References to the courses of study in science and mathematics at Oxford in the seventeenth century.

Richeson, A. W. "The First Arithmetic Printed in English," *Isis, 37* (1947), 47–56. A critical study of the first arithmetic (anonymous) printed in English.

Roberts, S. C. *British Universities* (London, 1947).

Ward, G. R. M. *Oxford University Statutes* (London, 1875). Volume 1 discusses many of the laws relating to the courses of studies offered in mathematics and science at Oxford University.

Watson, Foster. *The Beginning of the Teaching of Modern Subjects in England* (London, 1909). A history of the teaching of mathematics and science in England during the eighteenth century.

Yeldham, Florence. *The Teaching of Arithmetic Through Four Hundred Years (1535–1935)* (London, 1936).

Encyclopedias and Dictionaries

Edinburgh Encyclopedia, Conducted by David Brewster (London, 1819–1830), 18 vols. An authoritative reference source for eighteenth-century science.

Oxford English Dictionary (Oxford, 1933).

Real-Encyclopädie der classischen Altertumswissenschaft, ed. by Pauly-Wissowa (Stuttgart, 1905), Vol. 5. An excellent reference work for medieval science.

Rees, Adam E., ed. *The Cyclopaedia: or Universal Dictionary of the Arts, Sciences, and Literature* (London, 1819), 39 volumes of text and 6 volumes of plates. Extremely useful for work on technology. Contributors are not always identified.

Reisch, Gregor. *Margarita Philosophica* (Argentinae, 1504). An encyclopedia of the early sixteenth century giving examples of mathematical instruments. One of these, the polimetrum, was a prototype of the theodolite.

Index

"A" type frame, 2
Achromatic lens, 149, 164–166, 174, 196
Acre, 18, 19, 25, 36, 39, 109
Adams, George, 160
Agas, Ralph (Radulph), 81–83, 99
Agriculture, English, influence on surveying, 144, 145, 155
See also Enclosure system; Open-field system
Alidade, 47, 49, 84
American colonies, surveying in, 126, 127, 128, 129, 154, 163n, 201, 202
Apian, Peter, 9, 49, 53, 54, 56
Arabic influence, 23, 24, 26
Archimedes, 73
Architas, 73
Area measurement, Burgh's method of, 151–157, 203
Armillary sphere, 70
Astrolabe, 9, 11, 34, 49, 69, 70, 88, 196
Atwell, George, 120–122, 124, 125
Auzout, Adrian, 133, 134, 194

Babbage, Charles, 142
Bacon, Roger, 24, 130, 165

Balls of London, 120
Barthelet, Thomas, 31–33, 40–42
Beaumont College, Old Windsor, 26, 27
Bedwell, William, 47
Benese, Richard, 31, 35–42, 47, 71, 73, 79, 86, 94
Billingsly, Sir Henry, 47
Bird, John, 163–169 *passim*, 179, 187, 197–199, 205
Blagrave, John, 75n, 88
Bolingbrooke, barony of, 26, 27
Bourne, William, 47–52, 65, 69
Brahe, Tycho, 85, 87, 130, 132n
Brent, Charles, 150
Bretnor, Thomas, 91
Briggs, Henry, 104n
Burgh, Thomas, 151–157, 203
Burgis (Bruges), Roger, 104n
Burns, Arthur, 156, 158, 159, 200

Cambridge, England, survey of, 82n
Cambridge University, 23, 47n, 52, 91, 120
Carpenter's square, 53–56, 200
Cassini de Thury, César François, 176

INDEX

Celtic influence, 15
Chain, 104, 157, 174
   Gunter's, 107, 108, 115, 122,
      124, 125, 127, 129, 139–141,
      196
   Rathborne's, 108, 109, 115, 127,
      140, 141, 203
   steel, 178, 180, 183
Chain surveying, 34, 37, 120, 121,
   123, 125–126, 152–160, 200
Chanzler, Richard, 85, 87
Chaulnes, Duc de, 168, 169, 195
Chinese influence, 6, 193
Chorobates, 5, 136, 138
Christ College, Oxford, 109n
Circumferenter, 83, 93, 99, 100,
   106, 111, 114, 115, 127, 128,
   140, 153, 157, 173, 186, 203
Clark, Ernest, 32
Clavius, Christopher, 114
Close, Charles, 176
Cole, Humphrey, 11, 66, 67–70, 75,
   160, 186, 196
Compass, 6–8, 11, 30, 34, 49, 198
   beam, 141, 162, 179
   magnetic, 6, 7, 13, 14, 173, 175,
      193, 197, 199
Cord, 24, 34, 37, 54, 108, 140, 174
"Cosmographicall glasse," 195
Cosmography, books on, 9, 47
Crabtree, William, 133
Cross-staff, 53, 54, 57, 58, 84, 85,
   88, 200
Cruikshank, Joseph, 154
Cunn, Samuel, 146, 147, 150, 201
Cunningham, William, 47–48, 65
Curtius, Jacques, 130

Danfrie, Philip, 98
Davis, William, 157, 159
Dee, John, 44, 47, 52, 53, 65, 90
Diagonal scales, 84
Dial (dyall), 34, 69, 70
Digges, Leonard, 43, 44, 47, 52–
   67, 69, 70, 73, 74, 79, 82,
86, 88, 90, 92, 94, 95, 98,
   106, 130, 146, 160, 165, 186,
   196, 199
Digges, Thomas, 43n, 44, 58, 59n,
   74, 82n, 85–87, 90, 186
Dioptra, 4, 5, 13, 89, 195, 197, 198
Dividing, method of
   hand, 161–163, 166, 187, 197–199
   instrument, 166–172, 174, 187,
      197, 199
Dollond, John, 164, 165, 172, 174
Dollond, Peter, 164
Dudley, Robert, 84, 85
Dutch instruments, 165

Edward I (of England), 20, 25, 33
Egyptian influence, 3–6
Emerson, William, 144, 157, 159
Enclosure system, influence on
   surveying, 29ff., 128, 145,
   160
English instruments, 11, 88, 89,
   137, 172–174, 177
Epipedometron, 9
Euclid, 38, 46, 47, 73, 74, 114
Euler, Leonhard, 149n
European instruments, 6–13, 64,
   65, 84, 88, 89, 100, 137, 172
Eyre, John, 118–120, 140

Farmery, John, 81n
Field book, described, 111, 187,
   203
Fine, Grontius, 53
Fitzherbert, Sir Anthony, 22, 31–
   35, 36, 40, 41, 42, 71, 72, 73,
   77, 86, 189, 199, 201, 202
Fitzherbert John, 32, 33, 41, 189
Fitzherbert, Master, see Fitzher-
   bert, Sir Anthony
Fitzherbert, Reginald F. C., 32
Flamsteed, John, 146
Flemish influence, 7, 9, 53n
Foullon, Abel, 11–13

French instruments and systems, 22, 98, 177, 185
Furlongs (blocks of lands), 17

Galilei, Galileo, 131, 165
Gardiner, William, 147, 153–154, 159
Gascoigne, William, 132–134, 165, 192
Gay, Edwin F., 32
Gemini, Thomas, 69
Gemma Frisius, 9, 11, 13, 48, 49, 53, 203
Geometrical square, 53, 54, 59, 60, 62, 63, 88, 115, 200
Geometrical table, 70
Gibson, Robert, 154, 155, 159
Godwyn, John, 100
Graham, George, 161–163, 166, 179
Gray, John, 152, 153, 159, 203
Greek influence, 2–6, 23
Green, William, 165
Gresham College, Oxford, 109n
Grosseteste, Robert, 24
Gualterius Arsenius, 11
Gunter, Edmund, 109, 114, 115, 141
Gunter's chain, see Chain, Gunter's
Gunther, F. T., 9, 11, 65–69, 86, 164

Hall, Chester Moor, 149, 164, 165, 172
Hammond, John, 150, 201
Haskold, H. D., 146, 164
Heidelberg University, 47n
Henry VIII (of England), 64n
Hero of Alexandria, 4, 13, 89, 195, 197, 198
Herriot, Thomas, 44n
Hevelius, 134
Hindley, Henry, of York, 168, 169

Hirschvogel, August, 9n, 199
Holometer, 11–14, 173
Hooke, Robert, 134, 165–169
Hopton, Arthur, 95–103, 110, 111, 115, 139, 140
Horncastle, barony of, 26, 27
Hounslow Heath, survey of, 175, 177–185, 187, 188, 203
Husbandry, books on, 22

"Instrument geometricall," 53
Instruments
    angle-measuring, 152, 153, 155, 158–160, 165, 203
    line, 34, 140
    See also names of individual instruments
Isosceles, 2
Italian influence, 7

Jacob's staff, 84n
Jansen, Zacarius, 131
Jugge, Richard, 69

Kästner, A. G., 84
Kepler, Johannes, 132
Kirkstead Abbey, 26
Klingenstierna, S., 149n

La Hire, Philip de, 136
Lawrence, Edward, 147, 150, 151, 159
Leigh, Valentine, 31, 70–74, 77, 79, 94
Leroy, M. Julien, 167
Levels, 135–139, 149, 195, 197, 198
Levels and leveling, 135–139, 149, 195, 197
Levi ben Gerson, 84
Leybourn, William (Oliver Wallinsby), 103, 113–119, 122–124, 127, 128, 140, 186
    describes instruments, 114ff.
    textbooks by, 137, 138, 143, 146, 147, 150

Lincoln College, Oxford, 95n
Lippershey, Jan, 131
London, England, survey of, 82n, 104n
Louvain, University of, 53
Love, John, 114, 126–129, 140, 150
Lucar, Cyprian, 31, 75n, 77–81, 83, 202
Lyte, Henry, 91

Maps, 9, 69
Martindale, Adam, 92, 123–126, 205
Maskelyne, Nevil, 176
Mathematics, role of, *see* Table of Contents under Chapter Two: The Educational Movement; Chapter Five: Educational Background; Chapter Six: General Background
Measures, 17, 20, 25, 36
    perch, 17, 18, 36, 39, 40, 75n, 109
    pole, 17, 18
    rod, 17, 18, 25, 109, 140
    rood, 17
    ruthen, 25
    units of, defined, 36
Menna, Theban tomb of, 3
Mercator, Gerardus, 53
Merton, Augustine priory of, 35
Merton College, Oxford, 28
Micrometer, 132–134, 162, 165, 179, 187, 192
Microscope, 162
Montanari, Geminiano, 135, 165
Morin, Jean-Baptiste, 134

National Maritime Museum, Greenwich, England, 67, 68
Neale's Mathematical School for Boys, 146n
Neckham, Alexander, 6
Needham, Joseph, 6

Newton, Isaac, 149n
Nicholson, James, 35
Noble, Benjamin, 156, 157, 159
Nocturnal, 70
Nonius, 84, 85, 88, 130
Norden, John, 92–94, 99, 100, 139, 140, 150
Norman influence, 20, 24, 185, 191
Norwich, England, survey of, 47n
Norwood, Richard, 91, 92, 114
Nuñez, Pedro, 83, 84, 197

Oldenberg, Henry, 133
Open-field system, influence of, 17, 19, 29, 30, 144, 185
Ordnance Survey, 173, 175, 177, 200
Oxford, England, survey of, 82n
Oxford University, 23, 28, 35, 52, 66, 91, 95n, 109n, 164, 206

Padua, University of, 131n
Paris Observatory, 133
Paynell, Thomas, 35
Pearsall, A. W. H., 67
Peractor, 111, 203
Peregrinus, Peter, 6, 7
Picard, Jean, 133, 134, 146, 194
Pisa, University of, 131n
Piticus, 114
Plane table, 78–82, 88, 97, 98, 103, 104, 106, 111, 114, 115, 121, 125, 127, 140, 151, 153, 157, 173, 175, 198, 199, 202
Plow team, 16, 17
Plumb bob, 2, 5, 13, 135, 136
Pole, 54, 108
Polimetrum, 9, 10, 14, 64, 207
Porta, Giambattista della, 130, 165
Potter, Francis, 164
"Profitable staff," 53, 54
Protraction, 103, 110, 118, 121–123, 128, 129, 151

Puchner, 84
Purbach, Georg, 84, 86
Pyrometer, 172, 180

Quadrant, 47, 54, 64, 83–85, 164

Ramsden, Jesse, 149, 169–183, 187, 194, 197, 199
Ramus, Petrus, 47, 114
Rathborne, Aaron, 103–117, 123, 124, 127, 139–141, 186, 203
Read, John, Jr., 75n
Read, John, Sr., 75
Recorde, Robert, 44, 45, 47, 74, 75, 90, 92
Regiomontanus, 84, 86
Reisch, Gregorius (Gregor), 9, 10, 64
Reynolds, John, 75
Reynolds, Thomas, 69
Riccioli, Giovanni Battista, 136
Richard II, of England, 20
Riggs, J. M., 31
Rittenhouse, David, 165
Rod, 18, 24, 34, 174, 178–183
Roman influence, 2, 4–6, 13, 15, 16, 24, 191, 198, 200
Römer, Ole, 134
Rowley's bubble level, 138
Roy, William, 175–179, 181
Royal Observatory, Greenwich, 161, 176, 178
Royal Society of London, 133, 134, 177, 181
Roze (Rotz), Jean, 64
Rudolph II, Emperor, 132n

Saville, Henry, 91
Saxon influence, 16–20, 24, 25, 185, 191
Scales, 141
Scheiner, Christoph, 132
Schrivelsby, barony of, 26, 27
Scott, Dunbar, 65
Sector, 70, 141

Semicircle, 127
Sextant, 157, 195
Sidney Sussex College, Cambridge 91
Sisson, Jonathan, 139, 146–155 *passim*, 161, 163, 164, 166, 179, 187
Skeat, Walter W., 31, 191
Smeaton, John, 163, 168, 198, 199
Snell, Willebrord (van Roigen), 114
"Sphericall," 82
Spiedell, John, 91, 104n
Spirit level, 136–138, 193
Stadia, 135, 165, 166, 195, 197
Stave, 24
Stevin, Simon, 109
Sturmy, Samuel, 141
Sumerian instruments, 3, 4, 190

Talbot, Benjamin, 157
Tarbert Crinan lines, 165
Tartaglia, Niccolo, 7, 8, 48, 49, 100
Taylor, E. G. R., 11, 13, 45, 49
Telescope, 130–132, 135, 146, 149, 155, 164–166, 172, 187
Theodolite (theodelitus), 9, 157, 170, 178, 186, 195, 198, 203, 207
  altazimuth, 181–183
  of Bleau, 67
  Digges', 58, 59n, 60–62, 65–70, 82, 88, 93, 146, 196, 199, 200
  geodetic, 172
  Rathborne's, 103–106, 111, 114, 115, 127
  Sisson's, 147–149, 151, 153, 155, 201
Theodulus, 59n
Thevénot, Melchisédech, 136
Thompson, John, 75n
Tompson, Thomas, 161
Topographical glasses, 95–97, 103

"Topographicall instrument," 58, 59, 62–67, 82, 83, 86, 88, 98, 106, 140, 196, 200

Townley, Richard, 134

Transversals (traverse methods), 84, 85, 88, 103, 111, 180

Triangulation, use of, 50–52, 61, 89, 100, 101, 103, 145, 146, 157, 173–185, 187, 199, 203, 205

Trinity College, Oxford, 164

Troughton, Edward, 172, 199

Troughton, John, 163

University College, Oxford, 52

Vernier, 130, 134, 164, 187, 199

Vernier, Pierre, 130, 134

Vertical circle, 63

Vitruvius, 5, 136

Waldseemüller, Martin, 9, 10, 64

Wallinsby, Oliver, see William Leybourn

Walter of Henley, 22

Ward, Seth, 91

Water-level (instrument), 137

Watson, Foster, 45

Watson, Major General, 175

Watt, James, 165, 166, 197

Waywiser, 157

Wheel perambulator, 173, 194–199

Wildmore Fen, boundary dispute over, 26, 202

Wilson, Henry, 152, 153

Windsor, England, survey of, 92n

Wing, Vincent, 113n, 122, 123, 127, 141

Worsop, Edward, 46, 69, 74–77, 83, 86